# THE **MINI** ROUGH GUIDE TO
# VIENNA

T0015741

ROUGH
GUIDES

# YOUR TAILOR-MADE TRIP
## STARTS HERE

**Tailor-made trips and unique adventures crafted by local experts**

Rough Guides has been inspiring travellers for more than 35 years. Leave it to our local experts to create your perfect itinerary and book it at local rates.

Don't follow the crowd – find your own path.

## HOW ROUGHGUIDES.COM/TRIPS WORKS

**STEP 1** Pick your dream destination, tell us what you want and submit an enquiry.

**STEP 2** Fill in a short form to tell your local expert about your dream trip and preferences.

**STEP 3** Our local expert will craft your tailor-made itinerary. You'll be able to tweak and refine it until you're completely satisfied.

**STEP 4** Book online with ease, pack your bags and enjoy the trip! Our local expert will be on hand 24/7 while you're on the road.

# PLAN AND BOOK YOUR TRIP AT
# ROUGHGUIDES.COM/TRIPS

# HOW TO DOWNLOAD YOUR FREE EBOOK

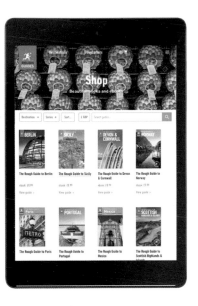

1. Visit **www.roughguides.com/free-ebook** or scan the **QR code** below

2. Enter the code **vienna431**

3. Follow the simple step-by-step instructions

For troubleshooting contact: mail@roughguides.com

# **10** THINGS NOT TO MISS

# A PERFECT DAY

### 9.00am

**Breakfast.** A hearty Alpine breakfast is a great set-up for the day, so eat your fill either from your hotel buffet (which is likely to include continental favourites such as bread rolls with butter and jam, slices of ham and cheese, boiled eggs, cereal, muesli and fresh fruit) or from the diet-busting breakfast menu at Café Drechsler, a longtime legend that today serves up pancakes, omlettes and even breakfast cocktails (see page 110).

### 10.00am

**Royal Palace.** Kick off your day of sightseeing at the Stephansdom with great city views from the tower; then take the U-Bahn southwest to Schloss Schönnbrunn, the Habsburg's baroque masterpiece. You'll just have time to take a tour of the 40 dazzling rooms before returning to the city centre.

### 12 noon

**Lunch.** Take your midday hunger pangs back to the Innere Stadt (see page 105) for some authentic, great value Viennese fare in Pfudl or go to Trzesniewski (see page 107) for a traditional open sandwich with lunchtime diners on the hop.

### 1.00pm

**Museum visit.** After lunch take the U-Bahn or tram to the famous MuseumsQuartier. MUMOK and Leopold Museum are top choices, and across the road stands the superb Kunsthistorisches Museum; you'd do well to spend time in any of them, but take your pick depending on taste. Cafés are plentiful too if you need to refuel.

# IN **VIENNA**

**Take a break.** You'll certainly be ready to take a break after all that walking and sightseeing, so now is a good time to hop across from the museum action into the Volksgarten for a quiet stroll, perhaps stopping off for a coffee at an open-air café.

**5.00pm**

**Mine's a *Beisl*.** Taking an early dinner frees up the rest of the evening for more Viennese experiences, so make your way to one of the city's friendly *Beisln*, a type of informal bistro with authentic local food and often with a cosy, darkwood interior. Beim Czaak (see page 105) or Reinthaler (see page 107) are popular with inner-city dwellers and are safe bets for finding good Austrian dishes like dumplings and schnitzel, as well as Palatschinken and Kaiserschmarren for desserts or sweet snacks.

**6.30pm**

**In a spin.** Next stop is the Prater amusement park for a spin on the big wheel, the Riesenrad, immortalised in the film *The Third Man*. If fun fairs are not your thing, there are plenty of Danube-side walks to take and parkland to explore, perhaps by bike.

**8.30pm**

**Tavern time.** A great way to round off the day is to head out of town to a *Heuriger* (wine tavern), perhaps Braunsperger (see page 109) or Fuhrgassl-Huber (see page 110) to sip some excellent local reds and whites as well as traditional food. They're easily accessible from the city centre.

# CONTENTS

# OVERVIEW

The sophisticated Viennese enjoy what is known as the *Wiener Lebensart*, a cultured appreciation of all life's pleasures. Not only is this reflected in Vienna's glorious art, music and architecture, theatres and coffee houses, and its passion for glittering balls, but where else would you find vineyards within a city's limits? The Innere Stadt (Old City) is a Unesco World Heritage Site (in addition to the Schloss Schönbrunn), a fitting honour for an area that embraces baroque palaces, the famous Burgtheater and Staatsoper (Opera House), and a warren of narrow medieval streets and lanes tangled around the Stephansdom (St Stephen's Cathedral).

Yet Vienna, with a population of over 2 million, has much to save it from becoming an open-air museum. Tired old sites are regularly revamped and given new uses, and various construction projects, from the whimsy of Hundertwasser's garbage incinerator to the steel Millennium Tower, add a 21st-century dimension. In the historic centre, projects such as the MuseumsQuartier blend old and new to bring fresh interest to the Austrian capital's cityscape. Vienna is divided into 23 districts. The 1st District is the historic Innere Stadt (Old City), and districts 2 to 9 fan out around the Ringstrasse.

## Viennese charm

The Viennese seldom miss an opportunity to make a flattering remark: 'I kiss your hand, Madam' or 'I am honoured'. Even the familiar greeting *'Servus'* ('hi' or 'bye') is Latin for 'your servant'.

Since the 16th century, Vienna has been universally acknowledged as Europe's capital of music. People come here to enjoy the waltzes of Johann Strauss – only he could have described the muddy brown Danube as blue – and baroque Mozart recitals at the Opera House. Visit the *Heuriger*

*Aerial view of the city at night*

wine garden on the edge of the Vienna Woods (Wienerwald) for a late-night glass of white wine and a few sentimental songs or knock back a couple of beers to something more modern in one of the city's clubs. And when all you want to do is kick back, Vienna is a city with space to relax, its rural setting inducing an easy-going attitude to life.

## TRADITION AND MODERNITY

The Viennese are proud of their city's heritage and achieve both continuity and change. Grand old hotels and coffee houses have been renovated, and the clientele – the artists, writers, thinkers and dreamers – have been joined by TV producers, business profession-als and, of course, tourists. Fashion designers have taken hold of the traditional *Loden* fabric and produced it in brighter hues to give a bit of oomph to the traditional olive-green jackets and overcoats, while the revered Burgtheater is constantly challenging opinions with provocative productions by the likes of Thomas Bernhard.

Urban transport

The Austrian capital also offers an astonishing range of museums, from the sublime to the surprising, from art and high culture to schnapps and reusable coffins (many of these can be visited for free or at reduced rates with the Vienna Card, available from the tourist information office). But some things don't change: *Fiakers* (carriages) still trundle tourists around the city centre; the pure white Lipizzaner stallions still prance at the Spanish Riding School; the Café Konditorei still lure customers with their creamy gateaux and the annual balls remain the focal point of the social calendar. The most glamorous event of the year however falls in February, when the Opera Ball brings hordes of artists, politicians and celebrities together at the State Opera House.

## AT THE CROSSROADS

Vienna's historic role as a crossroads of Eastern and Western European civilisation has taken on a new significance since the collapse of Soviet communism and Austria's entry into the European

Union in 1995. It's a veritable melting pot of cultures with a workforce made up of new generations of Poles, Italians, Turks, Croats and more.

The city's relaxed atmosphere often comes as a surprise to visitors and the Viennese still seem to have time for the courtesies of yesteryear. Although recent social innovations have been generally popular in Vienna, people remain profoundly conservative in their values. Politically the Viennese have always been impossible to define. They cheered their Habsburg emperors and then Napoleon. They welcomed the republican experiment after World War I, hailed Hitler, then found democracy rather to their liking as it seemed conducive to their legendary taste for *Gemütlichkeit*. Roughly translated, *gemütlich* means 'comfy and cosy', the quality that takes the rough edges off life. It is part of the famous Viennese charm, a charm also sharpened by undertones of sometimes malicious irony known as *Wiener Schmäh* (Viennese sarcasm).

## THE WALTZ

Music in Vienna is fuelled not only by its hallowed classical tradition, but also by the joy of its waltzes. The waltz began as a triple-time German traditional dance known as a *Ländler*, which the Viennese transformed into a whirling moment of fairyland. The man who brought the waltz to popular dance halls in 1819 was Joseph Lanner, leader of a small band. He took on a young viola player named Johann Strauss and the waltz took off in a big way. The group grew to become an orchestra and Strauss broke away to form his own – Lanner sadly celebrating the occasion with his *Trennungswalzer (Separation Waltz)*. The two conducted a prolonged 'waltz war' for public favour in the cafés of the Prater. The rivalry ended amicably and Strauss played waltzes – *adagio* – at Lanner's funeral.

# HISTORY AND CULTURE

From earliest times, Vienna was a crossroads for people migrating between Eastern and Western Europe. The first identifiable inhabitants of the area were Illyrians who sailed up the Danube from the Balkan Peninsula. Celts migrating from Gaul founded the town of Vindobona ('Shining Field') around 500BC.

## ROMANS AND BARBARIANS

The Romans arrived in the 1st century AD. Dispatched from Britain to shore up the empire's eastern European frontier, Rome's soldiers built their garrison in what is today the Inner City's Hoher Markt. They had their work cut out fending off invasions from the Teutons and Slavs. Emperor Marcus Aurelius led the fight against the barbarians, but died in Vindobona of the plague in AD180. A hundred years later, another Roman emperor, Probus, won the gratitude of subsequent generations by establishing vineyards on the slopes of the Wienerwald. Today, Probusgasse, a street in the heart of the *Heuriger* wine district of Heiligenstadt, honours his initiative.

Christianity arrived in the 4th century, but was powerless against successive waves of barbarian warriors. Attila the Hun advanced on Vienna in 453, but died before completing his conquest. The Huns were followed over the next 600 years by rampaging Goths, Franks, Avars, Slavs and Magyars. Despite these troubles, the first church, Ruprechtskirche, was erected in 740. Two more followed during the reign of Charlemagne: Maria am Gestade and the Peterskirche.

## BABENBERG RULE

Stability came in 1156 when the Babenbergs, Bavarian lords who had succeeded a century and a half earlier in driving out the

Magyars, were granted the hereditary duchy of Austria by the Holy Roman Emperor.

The first duke, Heinrich II Jasomirgott, set up his court around what is today the Platz am Hof, giving Vienna its first golden era. Art, trade and handicrafts thrived, attracting immigrant German merchants and artisans. Vienna became an important stopover for crusaders. Scottish and Irish monks on their way to Jerusalem founded the monastery of Schottenstift. Babenberg rule brought many new churches, notably the first Stephansdom, as well as several monasteries, elegant residences for the nobility along the broad new thoroughfares, and a fortress on the site of the future Hofburg castle. In 1200, financed with English ransom money paid to liberate King Richard the Lion Heart, a ring of fortifications was built around the Innere Stadt, along what is now the Ringstrasse.

It was also the great era of the minstrels and the start of Vienna's long musical tradition.

## THE HABSBURGS

In 1246, on the death of Friedrich der Streitbare (the Quarrelsome), the male line of the Babenbergs died out and the country fell to Ottokar II of Bohemia. Unlike his predecessor, who had disturbed the city's hard-earned peace by pick-ing fights with his barons, seducing the burghers' wives and going off to war

*Babenberg family tree at the monastery of Klosterneuburg*

## Obscure origins

For a dynasty that was to supply rulers to Germany, Austria, Hungary, Bohemia, Spain and other states, the Habsburgs had obscure origins. The house took its name from the castle of Habsburg, or Habichtsburg (Hawk's Castle), on the Aar River in present-day Switzerland, built by Werner, Bishop of Strasbourg, and his brother Count Radbot.

at the slightest provocation, Ottokar was popular with the Viennese. He made additions to the Stephansdom and started on the Hofburg. The people did not seem to appreciate that the new German king, Rudolf von Habsburg, had his eye on the city. They supported Ottokar, but in 1278 Rudolf triumphed.

Vienna's history for centuries thereafter was about constant confrontation between the Habsburgs' visions of grandeur and world conquest and the citizens' taste for the quiet life. Whenever the Habsburgs went about their empire-building, under Maximilian I, Karl V and Ferdinand I, Vienna was painfully neglected. The most popular rulers were the ones who chose to stay home and build things. Rudolf der Stifter (the Founder) created the university in 1365 and turned the Romanesque Stephansdom into the Gothic masterpiece you see today. Friedrich III finished the job and won Rome's approval for Vienna to become a bishopric in 1469. The Viennese showed their appreciation by burying him in the cathedral. As his tomb attests, it was Friedrich who dreamed up the grandiose motto: AEIOU, *'Austriae Est Imperare Orbi Universo',* for which the English translation is 'It falls to Austria to rule the world'.

The 15th century was not all sweetness and light: in 1421, more than 200 Jews were burned alive in their quarter around Judenplatz and the remainder were driven out of the city. The

Hungarian king Matthias Corvinus occupied Vienna from 1485 to 1490. He is remembered for his remark: 'Let others wage war while you, happy Austria, arrange marriages. What Mars gives to others, you receive from Venus.' The reference was to the Habsburgs' knack of expanding their empire through judicious mating of their innumerable archdukes and archduchesses, a policy that was used to great advantage by Maximilian I (1493–1519).

Picking up where the Goths and the Magyars left off, the Ottomans under Suleiman the Magnificent staged a crippling 18-day siege of Vienna in 1529. The suburbs were devastated, but the Innere Stadt held fast and the Turks were finally forced to retreat.

In the Reformation of the 16th century and the Thirty Years War that followed, the city emerged as a bulwark of the Catholic Church. Having withstood the Muslim Turks, Vienna banned Protestant worship in 1577, and repelled an attack by the Protestant Swedes of Gustav Adolph in 1645.

It was also during this time that Jews were allowed back into town, having been confined during the 1620s to a ghetto on the riverside marshlands of Leopoldstadt. Emperor Leopold I was the one to usher Vienna into its glorious baroque era, a veritable feast of architecture and

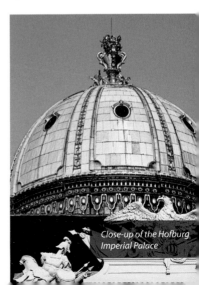

*Close-up of the Hofburg Imperial Palace*

music that scarcely paused to deal with the vicious plague of 1679 and another Ottoman siege in 1683. The great soldier and scholar Prince Eugene of Savoy was rewarded for his victory over the Turks with ample funds to build the magnificent and now renowned Belvedere Palace. The Auerspergs, Schwarzenbergs and Liechtensteins followed suit with palaces of a more modest, but equally elegant variety.

Karl VI, pretender to the Spanish throne, returned to Vienna more Spanish than Austrian, bringing with him the strict formality and piety of the Spanish court. His renovation of the 12th-century Abbey Klosterneuburg in baroque style was an attempt to create an Austrian version of El Escorial. Similarly, the huge Karlskirche was originally intended to emulate St Peter's in Rome. Vying with Versailles, the Hofburg Palace built the Spanish Riding School and the Imperial Library. The transformation of Vienna into a baroque city was largely the work of three Austrian architects: Johann Bernhard Fischer von Erlach, his son Josef Emanuel, and Johann Lukas von Hildebrandt.

## PRINCE EUGENE OF SAVOY (1663–1736)

Sceptical by nature, the Viennese have few authentic heroes; ironically, the greatest was a Frenchman who became the supreme Austrian patriot. A unique blend of military courage, culture and human warmth, Prince Eugene of Savoy was born in Paris in 1663. He arrived in Vienna in 1683, just in time to help out with the campaigns against the Turks. Over the next 30 years he fought brilliantly for Austria against the Ottomans and the French, rising to the position of commander-in-chief in 1697. Small of stature and always dressed in a simple brown uniform, he was known to his soldiers as 'the little Capuchin'.

## MARIA THERESA AND NAPOLEON

After the feverish construction projects that crowned the empire-building efforts of the male Habsburgs, the Viennese were delighted to be able to relax under the maternal eye of Empress Maria Theresa (1740–80). Pious, warm and sentimental, this mother of 16 children had an unerring feel for the moods of her capital's citizens. She was an enthusiastic patron of

*Empress Maria Theresa*

the arts, especially music. She loved to have concerts and operas performed at her newly completed Schönbrunn Palace, which she infinitely preferred to the more austere Hofburg. Her orchestra director was Christoph Gluck, a young Joseph Haydn sang in the Vienna Boys' Choir, and six-year-old Wolfgang Amadeus Mozart won Maria Theresa's heart by asking for the hand of one of her daughters (as fate would have it, the daughter in question, Marie-Antoinette, was destined to lose her head for somebody else). In the following years, these three composers – Gluck, Haydn and Mozart – launched Vienna's reputation as a city of music.

Whatever her virtues, it must be said that Maria Theresa lulled the Viennese into a false sense of security. Her son Joseph II (1780–90), very serious-minded and not particularly tactful, shocked them into a reluctant awareness of the revolutionary times that were coming. He rushed through a series of far-reaching reforms, making life easier for peasants, Protestants and Jews. But the

### Famous faces

Psychoanalyst Sigmund Freud, composer Gustav Mahler and playwright Arthur Schnitzler were all famous Viennese residents.

conservative Viennese were not ready. They were startled to see him open up the city by tearing down the wall around the Innere Stadt, and were dumbfounded by the bureaucratic machine he installed to run the empire.

People felt more secure with the cynical and not at all reform-minded Franz II, particularly following the news from France of the execution of Joseph's sister Marie-Antoinette. On seeing the strange tricolour flag hoisted by the new envoy of the French republic, the Viennese promptly tore it to shreds – along with diplomatic relations between Austria and France. They were less bumptious when Napoleon's armies arrived in November 1805 and the French emperor moved into Maria Theresa's Schönbrunn on his way to further glories at Austerlitz (in Moravia to the north).

Once more, the Habsburgs' secret weapon in foreign policy, politically astute marriages, came into play. Now, faced in 1810 with saving what was left of the empire, Emperor Franz did not hesitate to give his daughter Marie-Louise in marriage to his enemy Napoleon. The Viennese did not protest, preferring a peaceful life to more war.

## THE LONG 19TH CENTURY

The Napoleonic era ended with one of the city's most splendid moments, the Congress of Vienna in 1815, organised by Franz's shrewd chancellor, Metternich, for the post-war carving up of Napoleon's Europe. Franz was happy to leave the diplomatic shenanigans to Metternich while he supervised a non-stop spectacle of banquets, balls and concerts. Many considered Franz more successful than Metternich. 'This Congress does not make progress,' said Belgium's Prince de Ligne, 'it dances.'

For the next 30 years or so the city relaxed for a period of gracious living for the middle class and aristocracy, with the Prater park a favourite outing for royalty. And it was time for more music; Beethoven had become the darling of an aristocracy eager to make amends for its shameful neglect of Mozart. But in general the taste was more for the waltzes of Johann Strauss, both father and son.

In 1848 Vienna became caught up in a wave of revolution that spread across Europe in support of national independence and political reform. Ferdinand, the most sweet-natured but also the most dimwitted of Habsburg emperors, exclaimed when he heard that disgruntled citizens were marching on his Hofburg, 'Are they allowed to do that?' He fled town before getting an answer. The

*Johann Strauss the Younger
commemorated in the Stadtpark*

authoritarian Metternich was forced out of power, and the mob hanged the war minister, Theodor Latour, from a lamp post before imperial troops brutally re-established order.

Ferdinand abdicated and his deadly earnest nephew, Franz Joseph, took over. Grimly aware of his enormous burden, Franz Joseph concentrated throughout his 68-year reign on defending his family's interests and preserving as much of the empire as possible. Vienna offered him a paradoxically triumphant arena in which to preside over inevitable imperial decline. Prospering from the Industrial Revolution, the city enthusiastically developed the Ringstrasse, with imposing residences for capitalism's new aristocracy and expanded residential districts for the burgeoning bourgeoisie.

The World Fair in 1873, which nearly bankrupted the city, sang its praises, and people travelled from Europe and America to see the new opera house, concert halls and theatres. To a soundtrack by Brahms, Bruckner, Mahler, Lehar and Strauss the Austrian Empire's cultural achievements were consecrated in monumental form before the empire itself disintegrated. At the Secession Gallery, a group of young artists introduced a new style of art, which came to be known as *Jugendstil* (Art Nouveau). Only a spoilsport like Sigmund Freud over at the university would suggest that the Viennese examine the depths of their

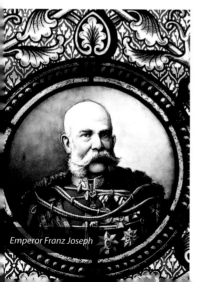

*Emperor Franz Joseph*

unconscious for the seeds of their darker impulses. They, of course, paid no attention. As the intellectuals in the coffee houses clucked disapprovingly, the town waltzed on. Meanwhile a would-be painter named Adolf Hitler quietly left town in disgust at this lack of seriousness, blaming the Jews and Slavs he had encountered in Vienna for the problems of the 'true Germans'.

## THE END OF THE EMPIRE

Having lost his son Rudolf through a suicide in Mayerling, and his wife Elisabeth to an assassin's knife in Geneva, Franz Joseph was stricken but fatalistic when he heard that his heir, Archduke Franz Ferdinand, had been shot in Sarajevo. The World War (1914–18) that followed ended the Habsburg Empire and left Vienna in economic ruin. Vienna lost its hinterland of Bohemia, Moravia, Slovakia, Hungary, parts of Poland, Romania and what was Yugoslavia, all of which had brought it economic prosperity.

Following World War I the state opera could boast Richard Strauss as its director, and the old creative spirit re-emerged in architecturally progressive public housing but the city suffered from crippling inflation. Politically polarised, street fighting broke out between Communists and Fascist supporters of the government of Engelbert Dollfuss. In 1934 Dollfuss was assassinated by the outlawed Austrian Nazis in the Chancellery on Ballhausplatz. His successor, Kurt von Schuschnigg, succeeded in crushing the putsch, but was forced four years later to yield to Hitler's *Anschluss* (German annexation) of Austria.

On 13 March 1938, Hitler's triumphant drive along the Mariahilferstrasse was cheered by the Viennese, who saw him as their saviour from the chaos of recent years. He proved the opposite for the city's 180,000 Jews. The brutality of the Austrian Nazis and the spite of many local citizens shocked even those who had witnessed their counterparts at work in Germany. The extermination of the Viennese Jews left a great stain on the city and a gaping hole in its intellectual life and cosmopolitan culture.

In some small measure, the city's spirit survived in World War II. Joseph Bürckel, the Nazi Gauleiter overseeing Vienna, warned Goebbels that it was perhaps better to allow satirical cabaret to continue. However, by the bombardments of 1945 all humour had evaporated. After the war, Vienna, like Berlin, was divided into four sectors, with the Innere Stadt under the joint administration of the Americans, Russians, British and French. The penury was countered by stoic acceptance and a vicious black market.

Austria's post-war neutrality, granted in 1955, made Vienna an appropriate host for the International Atomic Energy Agency, the United Nations Industrial Development Organisation and OPEC.

Austria joined the European Union in 1995, once more giving Vienna an active role in Europe. However, with the entry of a far-right party into the governing coalition, the country's reputation for unsavoury political attitudes again came under scrutiny, and the following years saw Austria enact some of the most restrictive immigration laws in the EU. The Viennese still cling to their social-democratic traditions, but Austria is split between left and right. Following the 2013 legislative election a grand coalition government ('Grosse Koalition') was formed by the left-wing Social Democratic Party of Austria and the right-wing Austrian People's Party. Today Politics in Austria still reflects the dynamics of competition among multiple political parties, which led to the formation of a Conservative-Green coalition for the first time in January 2020.

### No trace

Hitler's residence in the city is not commemorated. It is recorded that he stayed in a hostel at Meldemannstrasse 27 and that he had a flat at Stumpergasse 31. But there isn't anything to see at either site.

# HISTORICAL LANDMARKS

**c. 500 BC** Celts build town of Vindobona.

**1st century AD** Romans establish garrison.

**4th–9th century** Barbarian invasions.

**740** Ruprechtskirche is built, the earliest known Christian church.

**1156–1246** Babenbergs reign as dukes of Vienna; the first Stephansdom cathedral and precursor of the Hofburg castle is built.

**1278** Rudolf von Habsburg launches 640-year dynasty.

**1365** University of Vienna founded.

**1421** Jewish pogrom; 200 burned to death.

**1529** First Turkish siege repelled.

**1577** Catholic Church bans Reformation Protestants.

**17th C** Jews confined to ghetto and then allowed back into town.

**1683** Second Turkish siege repelled.

**1740–80** Popular Maria Theresa makes her home in Schönbrunn Palace; Haydn and Mozart make Vienna the musical capital.

**1780–90** Joseph II's reforms prove unpopular with the Viennese.

**1815** The Congress of Vienna carves up Europe while princes dance.

**1848** Short-lived revolt drives Metternich from Vienna. Emperor Ferdinand replaced by Franz Joseph (1848–1916).

**1873** World Fair celebrates Vienna's grandeur.

**1914–18** Defeat in World War I ends Austrian Empire.

**1934** Austrian Nazis assassinate Chancellor Dollfuss.

**1938** German annexation (*Anschluss*) of Austria.

**1939–45** World War II: Allied bombs devastate city.

**1955** Austria granted neutrality.

**1995** Austria enters European Union.

**2005** Austria celebrates *Jubiläumsjahr*, the 50th anniversary of the State Treaty and 60th of the Second Republic.

**2015** New laws ban foreign funding for mosques and imams.

**2020** Covid-19 pandemic takes hold in Austria and lockdown measures are implemented; Conservative-Green coalition formed for the first time.

**2023** Vienna celebrates the 150th anniversary of the 1873 Vienna World's Fair.

Vienna viewed from the steeple of the Stephansdom

# OUT AND ABOUT

Nearly all Vienna's major attractions are packed into the Innere Stadt (Inner City). This means that places such as the Stephansdom (St Stephen's Cathedral), the Hofburg (Imperial Palace), the Burgtheater (National Theatre), Mozart's house, the Staatsoper (State Opera) and the shopping areas around Kärntnerstrasse and the Graben are all within walking distance. Even the Kunsthistorisches Museum (Museum of Fine Arts) and Karlskirche are only just outside the Ringstrasse that marks the medieval precincts of the 1st District.

The best way to view the formidable monuments along the Ringstrasse is by tram (*Strassenbahn*; VRT, Vienna Ring Tram, runs around the Ring). Trams also cover some 28 routes to outlying districts and provide a good, cheap way of reaching other parts of the city on your trip, for instance Schönbrunn Palace or a *Heuriger* wine garden. The U-Bahn subway system has five lines, numbered U1 to U6 (U5 due to be built in 2026). U1 and U3 intersect in the city centre at Stephansplatz. The other most conveniently located station is Karlsplatz.

## INNERE STADT

### STEPHANSDOM

The imposing **Stephansdom** ❶ (St Stephen's Cathedral; Mon–Sat 6am–10pm, Sun 7am–10pm; free, charge for tours; www.stephanskirche.at), located right in the heart of Vienna, is the best place to start a tour. Whichever way you choose to walk through the Innere Stadt most inevitably gravitate towards the cathedral at some point. For more than eight centuries it has watched over Vienna,

### Secret code

Painted on the wall just inside the main entrance of the Stephansdom are the characters 05. This is the secret code of an Austrian resistance movement against the Nazis which began in 1944. The 5 stands for the fifth letter of the alphabet, E, and OE (Ö) is the first sound of Österreich (Austria).

enduring city fires, Turkish cannonballs and German and Russian shells. Part of the Stephansdom's charm derives from the asymmetry of its steeple, set to one side. Affectionately known as *Steffl*, it is 137m (449ft) high. Count 343 steps to the **observation platform** at the top, where the view extends northeast to the Czech Republic and southwest to the Semmering Alps.

The main portal takes its name, **Riesentor** (Giant's Gate), from a huge bone found during construction in the 13th century, which was thought to be the shin of a giant drowned in Noah's flood. Scientists subsequently concluded it was the tibia of a mammoth.

With its Romanesque western facade, Gothic tower and baroque altars, the cathedral epitomises Vienna's genius for harmonious compromise, here managing seamlessly to meld the austerity, dignity and exuberance of three architectural styles. The Romanesque origins (1240) are strikingly visible in the breathtaking **Heidentürme** (Heathen Towers) and statuary depicting, among others, a griffin and Samson fighting a lion. Above the entrance are Jesus, the Apostles and a veritable menagerie of dragons, lions, reptiles and birds representing evil spirits to be exorcised by the sanctity of the church.

The mainly Gothic structure we see today was built in the 14th and 15th centuries. To support their petition to have Vienna made a bishopric, the Habsburgs hoped to impress the Pope by adding a second tower. But the city fathers preferred to spend the money on strengthening city fortifications against the Turks and Protestants, so the **North Tower** was never properly completed, just topped off in 1578 with a frivolous Renaissance cupola. From atop the tower (accessible by lift) a fine view of the city opens up. In the tower swings the 20-tonne **Pummerin bell**, a recast version of the one made from the bronze of Turkish cannons captured after the 1683 siege, but destroyed in the wartime fire of 1945. It is only rung on special occasions such as New Year's Eve.

Inside the church, in the centre aisle, is the wonderfully carved Gothic **pulpit** by Master Anton Pilgram (1455–1515) At the head of the spiral staircase the sculptor has placed the figures of Augustine, Gregory, Jerome and Ambrose, fathers of the Church – and added a sculpture of himself looking through a window under

*The centre aisle and pulpit of Stephansdom*

*Stephansplatz and the Haas Haus*

the staircase. No shrinking violet, Pilgram pops up again at the foot of the elaborate stone organ base he built in the north aisle.

Left of the high altar is the carved wooden **Wiener Neustädter Altar**. To the right is the marble **tomb** of Emperor Friedrich III (died 1493), honoured by the Viennese for having the city made a bishopric and for inventing the *Semmel,* the little bread roll you receive with every meal.

Mass is held at 10.15am on Sunday and holidays (9.30am July and August). There are guided tours and roof walks, as well as tours of the bone-filled catacombs.

Opposite the Stephansdom looms the contrasting **Haas Haus**, a large, curved building whose windows reflect a distorted cathedral. This hinge between Graben and Stephansplatz was erected in 1990 to plans by Hans Hollein. Stephansplatz joins **Stock-im-Eisen-Platz** (literally meaning 'stick set in iron'), a name which refers to a gnarled old tree trunk on the corner of the Graben and Kärntnerstrasse into which journeymen locksmiths arriving in medieval Vienna would drive a nail for good luck. The nails are now protected by a Plexiglas shield.

## EAST OF STEPHANSDOM

If you're looking for a place to unwind after visiting the cathedral, walk east along Rotenturmstrasse to one of the outdoor cafés on **Lugeck**, a pleasant little square where burglars used to be hanged some 300 years ago. Or wander further over to the **Fleischmarkt**, where, at No. 11, you'll discover Vienna's oldest tavern, the **Griechenbeisl** (1490), once frequented by the likes of Mozart, Beethoven, Schubert, Strauss and Mark Twain, as well as by Marx Augustin.

Around the corner on Grashofgasse, cross the pretty court-yard of the 17th-century **Heiligenkreuzerhof** abbey, one of the Innere Stadt's most attractive nooks, to the **Basiliskenhaus** (Schönlaterngasse 7), steeped in medieval superstition. Here a basilisk – half rooster, half lizard – was said to have lived in a well and breathed its poisonous fumes into the drinking water, until one day a baker's apprentice held up a mirror to the monster and scared it to death.

From here it's a Mozartkugel's throw to the **Alte Universität** (Old University, 1365), where young Franz Schubert lived as a member of the Vienna Boys' Choir. The Alte Universität was closed down after student demonstrations in 1848 against the autocratic regime of Metternich, and the hotheads were moved out of the Innere Stadt to academies in the outer districts until a new university was opened in 1884, safely on the outer edge of the Ring.

On Bäckerstrasse, the baroque house of the old Schmauswaberl restaurant (No. 16) served students with leftovers from the Hofburg kitchens. The French lady of letters Madame de Staël lived at the Palais Seilern, and across the street (at No. 7) is a beautiful ivy-covered arcaded Renaissance courtyard.

## Du lieber Augustin

This famous Viennese folk song tells the story of a local itinerant bagpiper – Marx Augustin – who, while drunk late at night, fell into a pit filled with the bodies of dead plague victims, and lived to tell the tale.

Cut across the busy Wollzeile to **Domgasse 5**, where, from 1784 to 1787, Wolfgang Amadeus Mozart lived. The house is now a museum, the **Mozarthaus Vienna** ❷ (Tues–Sun 10am–6pm; U-Bahn 1, 3: Stephansplatz; www.mozarthausvienna.at), which was completely revamped and reopened in time for the 250th anniversary celebrations in 2006. Mozart wrote 11 piano concertos here, as well as one horn concerto, two quintets, four quartets, three trios, three piano sonatas, two violin sonatas and the opera *The Marriage of Figaro*. Just around the corner, in Rauhensteingasse, the composer struggled to finish the *Requiem* before his early death. His coffin was assigned to an anonymous grave in the St Marxer Friedhof.

Cheer up with a stroll through the **Fähnrichshof** at the corner of Blutgasse and Singerstrasse. This charming complex of artists' studios, galleries, boutiques, apartments and gardens is a triumph of urban renovation from the ruin left by World War II bombs. The nearby **Franziskanerplatz** presents a fine baroque ensemble – an 18th-century fountain with a statue of Moses by Johann Martin Fischer, the elegant **Franziskanerkirche** (Mon–Sat 7am–6pm) and the Kleines Café, tastefully remodelled by Hermann Czech.

# KÄRNTNERSTRASSE TO ALBERTINAPLATZ

Kärntnerstrasse was once the city's main north–south thoroughfare, continuing on through Carinthia (Kärnten) to Trieste on the Adriatic. It has always been the central artery of Viennese social life, perhaps because it joins the sacred and the cultural heart of Vienna – the Stephansdom at one end and the Staatsoper (Opera House) at the other.

The now transformed pedestrian zone street still contains some of Vienna's historic shops, such as Lobmeyr (No. 26) dating from 1823 and the Gothic Malteserkirche (No. 37), founded by the crusading Knights Hospitallers. Below the Steffl department store, **Mythos Mozart** (Mon–Fri 10am–8pm, Sat–Sun 10.15am–4.45pm; www.mythos-mozart.com), opened 2022, is a high-tech, multimedia experience dedicated to the musical genius. Just off Kärntnerstrasse, on Neuer Markt, is the **Kapuzinerkirche** (Church of the Capuchin Friars). Beneath it is the 17th-century imperial burial vault, the **Kaisergruft** (daily 10am–6pm; www.kaisergruft. at), also known as the Kapuzinergruft. Among the tombs and sarcophagi of some 140 Habsburgs, note the double casket of Maria Theresa and her husband, François de Lorraine. The most recent burial was in 1989, of Zita, wife of the last emperor, Karl I (who abdicated in 1918 and is buried in Madeira). Franz Joseph and Empress Elisabeth (Sissi) are apparently still much loved, their coffins festooned with flowers.

On Philharmonikerstrasse is the **Hotel Sacher** ❸, which opened in 1882. Anna Sacher, who presided over its early days, was a renowned hostess, anticipating her guests' every need. She attracted courtiers, aristocrats, diplomats and the rich, even embroidering their signatures on a tablecloth. The famous chocolate cake, the *Sachertorte*, is actually 50 years older than the hotel; it was created by Franz Sacher in 1832 for Prince Metternich when he wanted something new and impressive for an important occasion.

Lobmeyr on Kärntnerstrasse

At the intersection of Kärntnerstrasse and the Ringstrasse stands the **Staatsoper** ❹ (Opera House; guided tours various times depending on day of the week; www.wiener-staatsoper.at). The original Opera House, inaugurated in 1869, was greeted with such criticism that one of the architects, Edward van der Null, was driven to suicide. It was almost completely destroyed in the 1945 bombardments but rebuilt to the original design.

A lot about the opera's orchestra, from which the Wiener Philharmoniker is derived, can be learnt at the nearby **Haus der Musik** ❺ (Seilerstätter 30; daily 10am–10pm; U-Bahn 1, 3: Oper; tram 2, D, 71, VRT: Schwarzenberg Platz; www.hdm.at). Exhibitions are spread over three floors, of which the first has a display on the history of the Wiener Philharmoniker, with a 'compose your own waltz' game. Upstairs is the **Sonotopia**, an exploration of sound

*Bronze sculpture recalling Nazi oppression*

with fun interactive exhibits. The third floor has displays on some of the most famous composers to have worked in Austria.

Just beside the Staatsoper is **Albertinaplatz**. On the far side of the square is the Lobkowitz Palace, now home to the **Österreichisches Theatermuseum** (Wed– Mon 10am–6pm; U-Bahn 1, 2, 4: Karlsplatz; U-Bahn 3: Stephansplatz; tram D, VRT: Oper; www.theatermuseum. at). Inside are models of theatres, costumes and set designs, as well as the beautifully decorated Eroica Saal where Beethoven's Third Symphony was first performed. The museum's collection has been expanded to include the contents of the Staatsopernmusem, which closed in 2014.

*The Plague Column on the Graben*

Also on Albertinaplatz is the bleak **Monument against War and Fascism** (1991) by Alfred Hrdlicka. Facing the stone gate symbolising totalitarian force is the controversial bronze sculpture of a kneeling figure, recalling the humiliation of Jews forced by the Nazi regime to scrub pavements with a toothbrush.

Opposite the monument is the **Albertina ❻**, the Habsburg palace that contains the **Graphische Sammlung Albertina** (Albertinaplatz 1; daily 10am–6pm, Wed & Fri until 9pm; www. albertina.at). Named after Maria Theresa's son-in-law, Duke Albert of Saxony-Teschen, and founded in 1781, this palace holds one of the world's finest collections of graphic art, with more than 60,000 original drawings and over a million wood and copperplate prints. The collection showcases major artists from the 15th century to the present day, including priceless works by Dürer, da Vinci, Michelangelo, Raphael, Titian, Rembrandt, Rubens, Van Gogh, Toulouse-Lautrec, Beardsley and Grosz.

The state rooms have been restored in more recent times and an exhibition space created together with storage and retrieval facilities. Any of the drawings can be viewed by written request.

Just below the Albertina, with its entrance on Albertinaplatz, is Austria's **Filmmuseum** (Augustinerstrasse 1; call for opening hours; tel: 01 533 7054; www.filmmuseum.at), which puts on an exciting programme of art-house and period films, many taken from its comprehensive archive.

## THE GRABEN AND THE JEWISH QUARTER

Running northwest from Stephansplatz, the Graben, together with the adjacent Kohlmarkt and Dorotheergasse, is the centre of Vienna's most fashionable shops and coffee houses. Until the demise of the Habsburgs, it was equally infamous for its Graben nymphs, as the local ladies of the night were known. The Graben and its extension, Naglergasse, mark the southern boundary of the original Roman settlement of Vindobona; the approximate square shape is completed by Rotenturmstrasse to the east, Salzgries to the north and Tiefer Graben to the west.

The Graben is now a pedestrian zone, dominated by the startling, bulbous-shaped monument to the town's deliverance from the plague in 1679. The **Pestsäule** (Plague Column) combines humility before God and gruesome fascination with the disease itself. A more joyous celebration of faith, just off the Graben, is the **Peterskirche** ❼ (St Peter's Church; Mon–Fri 8am–7pm, Sat–Sun 9am–7pm; www.peterskirche.at), designed in 1702 by Gabriele Montani and completed by Johann Lukas von Hildebrandt. The exterior embraces the graceful oval of its nave, its rows of pews curving outwards, each decorated with three carved angels' heads. It displays the genius of Viennese baroque for marrying the sumptuous with the intimate.

South of Stephansplatz, at Dorotheergasse 11, is the **Jüdisches Museum ❽** (Jewish Museum; Sun–Fri 10am–6pm; U-Bahn 1, 3: Stephansplatz; www.jmw.at). The museum is housed in the 18th-century Palais Eskeles, formerly the property of a prominent Jewish financier. It traces the history of the city's Jewish community from the Middle Ages, through the years of its illustrious contributions to Viennese culture, to its extermination by German and Austrian Nazis in World War II. Temporary exhibitions are also staged here, usually devoted to prominent artists, writers and other historical figures of Viennese life. Despite the community's tragic end, the museum's approach is positive, reinforced by a cheery café and bookshop on the ground floor.

The old **Jewish Quarter**, still in large part a garment district, lies north of Stephansplatz and the Graben. Its medieval centre was **Judenplatz** (Jews' Square) until the pogrom of 1421, when the synagogue was dismantled and its stones carted off to build an extension to the Alte Universität. The remains of the synagogue have been excavated and now form

*The oval nave of the 18th-century Peterskirche*

Memorial to the Victims of the Holocaust

part of the elaborate **Museum Judenplatz Wien** (Sun–Thurs 10am–6pm, Fri 10am–2pm), which functions as an annexe to the Jüdisches Museum on Dorotheergasse. On the square is Rachel Whiteread's **Memorial to the Victims of the Holocaust**, which commemorates more than 65,000 Austrian Jews who were killed by the Nazis and is designed to resemble a library turned inside out, the shelves of closed books face inwards.

The one **synagogue** out of the city's 24 that survived the Nazis' 1938 *Kristallnacht* pogrom is at Seitenstettengasse 4, next to a kosher restaurant (guided tours Mon–Fri 10am; free). With its Jewish community centre, it stands behind an apartment block beside the unusual **Kornhäuselturm** (1827), studio and home of architect Josef Kornhäusel. Inside is a drawbridge he pulled up whenever he wanted to shut himself off from his quarrelsome wife.

Around the corner is the city's oldest church, the ivy-covered Romanesque **Ruprechtskirche** (opening hours erratic and likely to change at short notice), which is dedicated to Rupert, patron saint of salt – a valuable commodity in earlier times. From here, cut back through Judengasse to the **Hoher Markt**. This was once the forum of Roman Vindobona, and a small Römermuseum at No. 3 (Tues–Sun 9am–6pm; free entry on the first Sun of each month; www.wienmuseum.at) shows remains of two Roman houses laid bare by a 1945 bombardment. At the east end of the square is a gem of high Viennese kitsch, the **Ankeruhr**, an animated clock built in 1911 by an insurance company. Charlemagne, Prince Eugene, Maria Theresa, Joseph Haydn and others perform their act at midday.

At the western end of Hoher Markt, turn right into Marc Aurel-Strasse, named after the Roman emperor who died in AD 180. On the left, Salvatorgasse leads behind the **Altes Rathaus** (Old Town Hall), which now contains the **Archive of the Austrian Resistance** (Mon–Thurs 9am–5pm; www.doew.at), and past the superb porch of the **Salvatorkapelle**, a happy marriage of Italian Renaissance and Austrian late Gothic sculpture. Beyond it is the slender 14th-century Gothic church of **Maria am Gestade** (Mary on the Banks), originally overlooking the Danube. Notice its delicate tower, the canopied porch, and remains of Gothic stained glass in the choir.

## PLATZ AM HOF

Walk back across the Judenplatz to the spacious **Platz am Hof**, the largest square in the old part of the city. The Babenberg dukes, predecessors of the Habsburgs, built their fortress here in about 1150. It was both a military stronghold and a palace for festivities such as the grand state reception in 1165 for German emperor Friedrich Barbarossa. The **Mariensäule** (Virgin's Column) was erected in 1667 to celebrate victory over Sweden's armies in the Thirty Years War. It was on a lamppost in the middle of this square that the revolutionaries of 1848 hanged war minister Theodor Latour.

## Art forum

At Freyung 8, the Kunstforum der Bank Austria (daily 10am–7pm; www.bankaustria-kunstforum.at) mounts first-class exhibitions of contemporary art and sculpture, and paintings from the 19th and 20th centuries.

The end of the Holy Roman Empire, said by some to be neither holy nor Roman nor an empire, was proclaimed with fanfare at the baroque **Am Hof** church in 1806.

Along the narrow street to the left of the church is the **Uhrenmuseum** (Clock Museum; Tues–Sun 10am–6pm; free entry on the first Sun of each month; www.wienmuseum.at). Set in one of the oldest buildings in Vienna, with an attractive spiral staircase, it has some interesting exhibits (if you are into timepieces), including the huge workings of the original Stephansdom clock (1699) and the 18th-century astronomical clock made by the German watchmaker David Cajetano.

## AROUND HERRENGASSE

In Bognergasse, notice the pretty *Jugendstil* facade of the **Engel-Apotheke** (1907) before returning to medieval Vienna through narrow, cobbled Naglergasse. This leads to the **Freyung** triangle, flanked by the Palais Harrach dating from 1690 (where Joseph Haydn's mother was once the family cook; now a venue for temporary exhibitions mounted by the Kunsthistorisches Museum) and the **Schottenkirche** (Church of the Scots), founded by Scottish and Irish Benedictine monks in the 12th century, whose monastery has an excellent **museum** (Thurs & Fri 11am–5pm, Sat 11am–12.30pm & 1–5pm; www.schottenstift.at).

To the north of the Freyung, just before the Ringstrasse, Schottengasse leads to the Mölker Bastei and the **Pasqualatihaus**

(Tues–Sun 10am–1pm, 2–6pm; free entry on the first Sun of each month; U-Bahn 2, 4, tram 1, 43, 44, D, VRT: Schottentor; www.wienmuseum.at). Beethoven lived in this house on several occasions between 1803 and 1815 at the invitation of his friend and patron, Baron Johann Baptist of Pasqualati. Here he composed parts of *Fidelio* and his Fourth to Seventh symphonies, as well as his Piano Concerto in G-major (Opus 58). Today it is one of three Beethoven residences in Vienna open to the public as museums (see pages 74 and 77).

South of the Freyung is Herrengasse, the Innere Stadt's main eastbound traffic artery, lined with imposing baroque and neo-baroque palaces, now serving as government offices or embassies. Here, too, stands the 18th-century **Palais Ferstel**, incorporating an elegant shopping arcade, Freyung Passage, and the renovated

*Relaxing in Café Central*

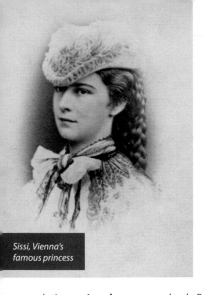

*Sissi, Vienna's famous princess*

**Café Central**, Vienna's leading coffee house before World War I (see page 110). Upstairs, a restaurant occupies the gilded premises of the old stock exchange.

Herrengasse leads to Michaelerplatz and the Hofburg. Once the imperial parish church, **Michaelerkirche** (Mon–Sat 7am–10pm, Sun and holidays 8am–10pm) is a hybrid mixture of Romanesque, Gothic and baroque. At No. 5 is the architecturally revolutionary **Looshaus**, now a bank. Built by Adolf Loos, its starkly functional use of fine materials shocked many in 1910. Emperor Franz Joseph so hated its 'outrageously naked' facade that he stopped using the Hofburg's Michaelertor exit.

## THE HOFBURG

Defeat in war took away the Habsburgs, but not the palaces. The most imposing is the **Hofburg** ❾ (Michaelerplatz 1; U-Bahn 2: Babenbergerstrasse or Herrengasse; tram 1, 2, D, VRT: Burgring), home of Austria's rulers since the 13th century.

Covering the southwest corner of the Innere Stadt, the vast palace went through five major stages of construction over six centuries, and at the end there was still a large unfinished section. Today, the palace's museums exhibit most of the vast personal fortune of the Habsburgs.

## IMPERIAL APARTMENTS

To sense the human scale of the gigantic enterprise, start by taking the 45-minute guided tour of the **Kaiserappartements** (Imperial Apartments; daily 9am–5pm; www.sisimuseum-hofburg.at). Coming from the Michaelerplatz, the entrance is to the left of the Hofburg rotunda. You will see splendid Gobelins tapestries; a smoking room for the emperor's fellow officers; enormous rococo stoves needed to heat the place; a crystal chandelier weighing half a tonne; Franz Joseph's austere bedroom with iron military camp-bed; and rooms used by his wife, Elisabeth (Sissi), including her newly restored drawing room and bedroom, and the gymnasium she used for daily exercise, complete with wall bars and climbing ropes.

### THE LIFE AND DEATH OF AN EMPRESS

Elisabeth, affectionately known as Sissi, was a Bavarian princess and a legend both in her own lifetime and more than a century after her death. Married to Emperor Franz Joseph 1 in 1854 when she was just 16, she was never at home with the oppressive formality of court life, but her presence still made the court the most glittering in Europe. She was noted for her stringent exercise and beauty regime (she spent hours on her hair), and her hairdresser was a confidante who sometimes took her mistress's place during boring functions where the empress would not be closely scrutinised.

As she grew older, Sissi was able to lead her own life, travelling extensively which gave her a love for the imperial train. In 1898, at the age of 60, she was fatally stabbed by an Italian anarchist in Geneva. In Austria and Hungary she is still a figure of enchantment; a Winterhalter portrait of Sissi with stars in her hair, old romantic films and, most recently, a musical about her life have, perhaps, kept memories fresh.

The first six rooms, the so-called Stephansappartement, are devoted to the **Sissi Museum**. This examines the life of the empress from her carefree childhood in Bavaria to her murder at the hands of an anarchist in Geneva. Particular emphasis is placed on the private life of Elisabeth, including her obsessive exercise regimes and fixation with beauty.

## SILVER COLLECTION

To the right of the Hofburg rotunda coming from the Michaelerplatz is the **Hofsilber und Tafelkammer** (Imperial Silver and Tableware Collection; same times as the Imperial Apartments). On display are the priceless Chinese, Japanese, French Sèvres and German Meissen services amassed by the Habsburgs over six centuries of weddings and birthdays. Highlights include a 140-piece service in vermeil and a neo-Renaissance centrepiece given to Emperor Franz Joseph by Queen Victoria in 1851.

## THE STALLBURG

In 1533, four years after the Turks were repulsed, Ferdinand I felt safe enough to settle in the Hofburg, bringing his barons and bureaucrats to make their homes in nearby Herrengasse and Wallnerstrasse. He built the **Stallburg** in 1565 (outside the main Hofburg complex on Reitschulgasse) as a home for his son Archduke Maximilian, subsequently turned into stables for the Spanish Riding School. With its fine three-storey arcaded courtyard, the Stallburg is the most important Renaissance building in Vienna. After an outbreak of infection some years ago the stables are no longer open to the public.

## SPANISH RIDING SCHOOL

Part of the massive expansion of the Hofburg that took place in the 17th and 18th centuries is the magnificent parade hall of the

**Winterreitschule**, home of the **Spanische Reitschule** ❿ (Spanish Riding School), right opposite the Stallburg. It is worth visiting on architectural grounds alone: constructed between 1729 and 1735, it is the work of Josef Emanuel Fischer von Erlach and is considered a masterpiece of the baroque era.

The Lipizzaner horses perform in its elegant arena throughout the year, except in January and July. Tickets must be booked well in advance (performances Sat and/or Sun 11am; guided tours daily; www.srs.at; performances can be booked in advance online, and the daily schedule is posted on leaflets outside the entrance under the Michaelertor). A cheaper option is to watch the horses train. Morning exercises are usually held between 10am and 11am Tuesday to Friday (with some exceptions) except in July; tickets can be booked online.

The Great Hall of the National Library

The Lipizzaners, originally a Spanish breed, were raised at Lipica in Slovenia, not far from Trieste; since 1920 the tradition has been carried on in the Styrian town of Piber. Using methods unchanged since the 17th century, the horses are trained to perform complex steps and dances.

## NATIONAL LIBRARY

Beside the Spanish Riding School complex is **Josefsplatz**, a marvellously harmonious baroque square, in the middle of which

*The Vienna Boys' Choir sings in the Schweizerhof*

stands Franz Anton Zauner's equestrian statue (1795–1807) of Emperor Joseph II.

Behind stands the main building of the **Österreichische Nationalbibliothek** ⓫ (Austrian National Library), which contains more than 2 million manuscripts and printed books, as well as maps, portraits, musical scores, papyrus documents and a globe museum. The building – the former Imperial Library – is one of the most important works of the court architect Johann Bernhard Fischer von Erlach, but it was built between 1723 and 1735 under the supervision of his son, Josef Emanuel. The highlight is the **Prunksaal** (Great Hall; Fri–Wed 10am–6pm, Thurs 10am–9pm, Oct–May closed Mon; www.onb.ac.at), one of the world's greatest secular baroque interiors. The ceiling frescoes (1730) by Daniel Gran depict the apotheosis of the library's founder, Emperor Charles VI.

The baroque **Augustinerkirche** was traditionally the Habsburgs' wedding church. It was here that Maria Theresa married François of Lorraine in 1736, Marie-Louise married Napoleon *(in absentia)* in 1810, and Franz Joseph married Elisabeth in 1854. Although the Habsburgs' burial church is the Kapuzinerkirche over on Neuer Markt, the heart of the deceased was buried deep in the Augustiner crypt.

## SCHWEIZERHOF

The **Schweizerhof** (Swiss Court), the oldest part of the Hofburg, is named after the Swiss Guard that was once housed there. It was here King Ottokar of Bohemia built a fortress in 1275 to resist Rudolf von Habsburg. Victorious Rudolf moved in and set about strengthening the fortifications to keep out the unruly Viennese; you can still see the pulleys for the chains of the drawbridge by the archway. But Rudolf's son, Albrecht I, preferred the safety of Leopoldsberg in the Vienna Woods. For 250 years, the fortress was used only for ceremonial occasions. The **Burgkapelle** (Castle Chapel; Sept–June Mon–Tues 10am–2pm, Fri 11am–1pm; www.hofmusikkapelle.gv.at) was built in 1449. Originally Gothic, it was redone in baroque style and then partially restored to its original form in 1802.

### VIENNA BOYS' CHOIR

The Wiener Sängerknaben (Vienna Boys' Choir) was founded in 1498 as part of the Imperial Chapel choir with 16 to 20 choirboys. It increased steadily in size over the years, and in the 18th and 19th centuries included Josef Haydn and Franz Schubert among its members. Re-established in 1924, it today consists of four individual choirs, each having 24 members. The choir sings Mass on Sunday and at Church festivals in the Burgkapelle (www.wienersaengerknaben.at).

*The imperial crown*

In the Schweizerhof, the **Schatzkammer** 🄬 (Treasury; Wed–Mon 9am–5.30pm; www.khm.at) contains a dazzling display of the insignia of the old Holy Roman Empire. Highlights are the imperial crown of pure unalloyed gold set with pearls and unpolished emeralds, sapphires and rubies. First used in AD 962 for the coronation of Otto the Great in Rome, it moved on to Aachen and Frankfurt for crowning successors. Also on display are the sword of Charlemagne and the Holy Lance, which is said to have pierced the body of Christ on the Cross and which has been claimed by some, including Hitler, to have mystical powers. Other intriguing artefacts include a unicorn's horn and an agate bowl, reputed to be the Holy Grail used by Christ at the Last Supper.

## IN DER BURG

The Schweizertor (Swiss Gate) leads into the busy square known as **In der Burg**, which is surrounded by buildings from various eras. Leopold I launched the city's baroque era with his **Leopoldinischer Trakt** (Leopoldine Wing) – a residence in keeping with the Habsburgs' role as a world power. Constructed in 1660–66 by Domenico and Martin Carlone, to a design by Philiberto Luchesi, it serves today as the official residence of the president of Austria.

The **Amalienburg**, which was started under Emperor Maximilian II in the early baroque style, was finished in 1611 during the reign of Emperor Rudolf II by Pietro Ferrabosco and Antonio de Moys. It was named after Amalia of Brunswick, the consort of Emperor Joseph I.

The **Reichskanzleitrakt** housed the imperial administration until 1806. It was designed by Johann Lukas von Hildebrandt and Josef Emanuel Fischer von Erlach between 1723 and 1730; the four sculptures *(The Labours of Hercules)* are the work of Lorenzo Mattielli, who was active at the same time.

## NEUE BURG

A passage leads from In der Burg to spacious **Heldenplatz** ⓭ (Heroes' Square). At the end of the 19th century, Franz Joseph embarked on building a gigantic Kaiser Forum. This was to have embraced the vast Heldenplatz with two crescent-shaped arms, the whole extending through triumphal arches to the Naturhistorisches and Kunsthistorisches

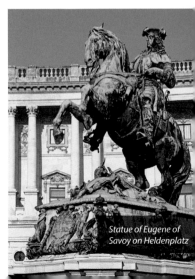

*Statue of Eugene of Savoy on Heldenplatz*

museums. Only the first of the two crescents, the **Neue Burg**, was built before the empire collapsed. Today, it houses a congress centre, several museums, and reading rooms for the National Library.

The building contains perhaps the most Viennese of all collections in the Hofburg, the exquisite **Sammlung alter Musikinstrumente** (Period Musical Instruments Collection; Thurs–Mon 10am–6pm, Tues 10am–9pm; www.khm.at), comprising some 360 pieces, including Renaissance instruments representing practically everything blown, strummed or tinkled up to the 17th century. Also on display are Haydn's harpsichord, Beethoven's piano of 1803 and an 1839 piano used by Schumann and Brahms.

The other museums in the Neue Berg are the **Hofjagd und Rüstkammer** (Collection of Arms and Armour; Thurs–Mon 10am–6pm, Tues 10am–9pm; www.khm.at) and the **Ephesos Museum** (Tues–Sun 10am–6pm, Thurs 10am–9pm), with exhibits from excavations at the site in Turkey. The star attraction is the **Weltmuseum Wien** (Thurs–Mon 10am–6pm, Tues 10am–9pm; www.weltmuseumwien.at), the ethnographic collections of the Habsburgs.

## THE BURGGARTEN

The **Burggarten**, the Hofburg's park, was laid out for the imperial family in the early 19th century. It has monuments to Franz Joseph I (1908, by Klimbusch) and Mozart (1896, by Viktor Tilgner), the latter moved here from Albertinaplatz in 1953. There is also the early 20th-century *Jugendstil* Palmenhaus (Glass House) by Friedrich Ohmann. This contains a lovely café, and the Schmetterlinghaus, a butterfly garden (Apr–Oct Mon–Fri 10am–5pm, Sat–Sun 10am–6pm, Nov–Mar daily 10am–4pm; www.schmetterlinghaus.at).

# RINGSTRASSE AND ITS MUSEUMS

After the Hofburg, take a walk (or tram ride) around the Ringstrasse, the single urban achievement of Franz Joseph I. This boulevard, encircling the Innere Stadt, was created in the 1860s along the route of the old city walls.

Start west of the Schottenring, at the **Votivkirche** (Tues–Sat 11–5pm, Sun 9am–1pm), a neo Gothic church built after Franz Joseph survived an assassination attempt in 1853. Next to it are the university and **Rathaus** (Town Hall). Proceed along Universitätsring, and on the Innere Stadt side is the imposing **Burgtheater**, a high temple of German theatre. Beyond is the lovely **Volksgarten**, with its small buildings and scaled-down copy of the Athenian Temple of Theseus. Its cafés and concerts carry on

*Maria-Theresien-Platz and the Kunsthistorisches Museum*

Inside the
Kunsthistorisches Museum

a tradition that began with the café music of the Strauss family.

Opposite rises the temple-like **Parlament**, built by Theophil Hansen after a long sojourn in Athens. The ring then curves round to become the Burg Ring, flanked on the Innere Stadt side by the Hofburg and on the other side by **Maria-Theresien-Platz**, which lies between the Kunsthistorisches Museum and Naturhistorisches Museum.

## KUNSTHISTORISCHES MUSEUM

If the **Kunsthistorisches Museum** ⓮ (Museum of Fine Arts; Tues–Sun 10am–6pm. Thurs until 9pm; U-Bahn 3: Volkstheater; tram 1, 2, D, VRT: Burgring; wheelchair access Burgring 5; www.khm.at) is less well known than the Louvre or the Prado, it may just be that the name is something of a mouthful. The collection, celebrating its 125th anniversary in 2016, is, quite simply, magnificent. Benefitting from the cultural diversity of the Habsburg Empire, it in fact encompasses a much broader spectrum of Western European art than many of its better-known counterparts. The **Gemäldegalerie** (Gallery of Paintings) on the first floor displays a dazzling array of European art from the 16th to 18th centuries. Dutch, Flemish, German and English works are in the east wing, left of the main entrance, and Italian, Spanish and French works in the west wing, to the right. You can't fail to be awestruck: there are masterpieces by Caravaggio, Dürer, Raphael, Rembrandt, Rubens, Titian, Velázquez, Vermeer, and an entire room devoted to Pieter Brueghel.

The lower floor contains an impressive, and beautifully displayed, collection of ancient Egyptian, Greek and Roman art, as well as the **Sculpture and Applied Arts Collection**, where the prized possession is Benvenuto Cellini's famous gold-enamelled **salt cellar** made for King François I of France. A highlight of the **Classical Antiquities Collection** is the exquisite **Gemma Augustea**, a 1st-century AD onyx cameo. The **Egyptian/Oriental Collection** contains, among other treasures, the burial chamber of Prince Kaninisut.

## NATURHISTORISCHES MUSEUM

The architectural twin of the Kunsthistorisches Museum stands opposite: the **Naturhistorisches Museum** (Natural History Museum; Thurs–Mon 9am–6pm, Wed 9am–8pm; U-Bahn 2, 3: Volkstheater; tram 1, 2, D, VRT: Dr Karl-Renner-Ring; www.nhm-wien.ac.at). The museum contains exhibits ranging from insects to dinosaurs, and an impressive collection of meteorites. The vast reserves derive in part from the private collections of François of Lorraine (1708–65), husband of Maria Theresa. Highlights include the 25,000-year-old figurine *The Venus of Willendorf*, a 117kg (260lb) giant topaz, and Maria Theresa's exquisite jewel bouquet made of precious stones.

## MUSEUMSQUARTIER

At the other side of Museumstrasse is the modern museum complex, the **MuseumsQuartier** ⓯ (Visitor and Ticket Centre, Museumsplatz, daily 10am–7pm; U-Bahn 2, 3: Volkstheater; www. mqw.at). Comprising Fischer von Erlach's 18th-century former

*Relaxing outside MUMOK*

Hofstallungen (Imperial Stables) alongside stunning new buildings, it is home to **MUMOK** (Museum of Modern Art, Tues–Sun 10am–6pm; www.mumok.at), with its fine collection of 20th-century work by artists such as Kandinsky, Magritte and Warhol; the superb **Leopold Museum** (Wed–Mon 10am–6pm; www.leopoldmuseum.org), featuring a wide selection of Austrian art dating from the 19th and 20th centuries and including works by Klimt, Schiele and Max Oppenheimer; and the **Architekturzentrum Wien** (Vienna Architecture Centre; daily 10am–7pm; www.azw.at), which, aside from a great café, hosts inspiring temporary shows. Contemporary art exhibitions can be viewed at the **Kunsthalle Wien** (Tues–Sun 11am–7pm, Thurs until 9pm; www.kunsthallewien.at). The **Tanzquartier** (Mon–Fri 9am–7.30pm, Sat 10am–7.30pm; www.tqw.at) is one of Europe's most important contemporary dance centres with performances, workshops, lessons and other dance-related events taking place (see website for programme).

## FINE ARTS ACADEMY

The Ringstrasse gradually bends round to become the Opern Ring. On the right is Schillerplatz, home to the **Akademie der Bildenden Künste** (Academy of Fine Arts; Tues–Sun 10am–6pm; U-Bahn 1, 2, 4: Karlsplatz/Oper; tram 1, 2, D, VRT: Burgring; www.

akademiegalerie.at). Few art academies can rival its outstanding collection of European paintings – particularly Dutch and Flemish masters – from the 14th century to the present day. Highlights include *The Last Judgement* by Hieronymus Bosch and works by Rubens, Rembrandt, Van Dyck, Pieter de Hooch and Tiepolo. The building itself was constructed in the 1870s to an Italian Renaissance design by Theophil Hansen.

## SECESSION BUILDING

Standing defiantly opposite, on the corner of Friedrichstrasse, is the distinctive **Secessionsgebäude** ⑯ (Secession Building; Tues–Sun 10am–6pm; U-Bahn 1, 2, 4: Karlsplatz; tram 1, 2, D, VRT:

### JUGENDSTIL

In Austria, *Jugendstil* (Art Nouveau) caught the imagination of the art world, and the result was the foundation of the Secession Movement by a group of renegade artists from the Academy in 1897. The central figure of the Secession was Gustav Klimt (1862–1918), whose erotic, fairytale-like painting and themes came to embody *Jugendstil*. One of the key tenets for artists such as Klimt and Koloman Moser, and the leading *Jugendstil* architects Otto Wagner and Josef Hoffmann, was the linking of function and aesthetic.

Klimt's decorative elegance was a particular source of inspiration for Egon Schiele (1890–1918), whose linearity and subtlety reveals the strong influence of the *Jugendstil*. Schiele, however, emphasised expression over decoration, concentrating on the human figure with an acute eroticism that was less decorative than Klimt's. Evocation of intense feeling through colours and lines was of equal importance to Oskar Kokoschka (1886–1980), a leading exponent of Expressionism.

_The Secession Building_

Burgring; www.secession.at). This is the gallery of the Secession Movement, which was formed when 19 artists (the most celebrated being Gustav Klimt) broke from what they saw as the reactionary Viennese art establishment in 1897. It was built by Josef Maria Olbrich, a student of Otto Wagner. An inscription above the door proclaims: _'Der Zeit ihre Kunst, der Kunst ihre Freiheit'_ ('To the Age, its own Art; to Art, its own Freedom'). The building is topped with a golden dome of laurel leaves, known locally as the 'golden cabbage', and said to symbolise the interdependence of art and nature. Contemporary work is also on show. In the basement is Klimt's large Beethoven Frieze, created for a Secession exhibition in 1902.

## KARLSPLATZ

There are a number of attractions on and around nearby **Karlsplatz** ⓱. The elegant glass cube on Treitlstrasse is the **Kunsthalle Project Space** (Tues–Sun 11am–7pm, Thurs until 9pm; U-Bahn 1, 2, 4: Karlsplatz; www.kunsthallewien.at), a branch of the Kunsthalle Wien (in the MuseumsQuartier), which stages exhibitions featuring topical themes and current trends in contemporary art. The café, with its giant terrace, is a favourite meeting place come night-time.

The square is dominated by the huge **Karlskirche** (Mon–Sat 9am–6pm, Sun noon–7pm), the most important of the city's baroque churches. It was built by Fischer von Erlach for Karl VI, fulfilling an oath made by the emperor during the plague of 1713. Sunset offers a spectacular view of the big dome across Karlsplatz. The cool, sober interior has a subdued marble decor and spacious oval ground plan similar to that of the Peterskirche. The oval dome's ceiling **frescoes** are by Johann Michael Rottmayr, the *trompe-l'oeil* by Gaetano Fanti. Notice, too, Daniel Gran's lovely painting of **St Elisabeth** in the main chapel on the right. In front of the church, Henry Moore's sculpture *Hill Arches* provides a striking contrast.

At the eastern end of Karlsplatz is **Wien Museum Karlsplatz** (closed for renovation and expansion until December 2023; U-Bahn 1, 2, 4: Karlsplatz; www.wienmuseum.at). Displays cover the major historical events in the city, from the siege of 1529 to *fin*

*Stadtbahn Pavilion by Secession architect Otto Wagner*

*The Musikverein*

*de siècle* artistic movements, including a re-creation of the living room of architect Adolf Loos. There are fascinating models of the city before and after the development of the Ringstrasse.

Opposite is the magnificent neoclassical building of the **Musikverein** (Society of the Friends of Music; check website for guided tour dates and times; www.musikverein.at). Constructed in 1867 to a design by Theophil Hansen, it is home to the world-famous Vienna Philharmonic Orchestra. The ceiling paintings, *Apollo and the Nine Muses* (1911), are by August Eisenmenger.

Beside the Musikverein lies the **Künstlerhaus** (1868), which houses art exhibitions (daily 10am–6pm; www.k-haus.at). In front are Otto Wagner's **Stadtbahn Pavilions** (Municipal Railway Pavilions), with their graceful green, gold and white motifs of sunflowers and tulips. Across the Kärntner Ring, the road becomes the Schubert and then the Park Ring as it barrels past the **Stadtpark**, home to the famous gilded bronze and marble monument to Johann Strauss the Younger.

## APPLIED ARTS MUSEUM

On the same side of the Ring, across Weiskirchnerstrasse is the **Museum für Angewandte Kunst** ⓲ (Museum for Applied Arts; Wed–Sun 10am–6pm, Tues 10am–9pm; U-Bahn 3, tram 2, VRT:

Stubentor; U-Bahn 4: Landstrasse; www.mak.at). Known simply as MAK, this is one of the city's most exciting and thought-provoking museums. The exhibition spaces are designed by contemporary artists who often reveal unexpected sides to quite mundane objects, such as the shadow play on Michael Thonet's bentwood chairs; you'll never view dining chairs in quite the same way again. There's a chance to see some particularly fine Viennese Biedermeier furnishings, as well as a collection of East Asian and Islamic art. The unmissable museum shop has a selection of items – design-conscious, arty and some downright humorous.

Opposite the museum lies Dr Karl Lueger-Platz with its memorial to Dr Karl Lueger, the populist – and anti-Semitic – mayor of Vienna

## BIEDERMEIER

The architecture, furniture and interior decoration known as 'Biedermeier' was produced in the period following Napoleon's defeat, between the Congress of Vienna in 1815 and the revolution in 1848. It was a time of political suppression in which the middle classes turned their attention to the arts. Biedermeier began as a satire, poking fun at the plodding German middle class. Two authors, Ludwig Eichrodt and Adolf Kussmaul, wrote poems in a journal called *Fliegende Blätter*, purporting to be the works of the unsophisticated 'Biedermeier', who, with his chum 'Bummelmeier', were boringly conventional. The name became synonymous with the age, but the work produced was far from dull. The Villa Wertheimstein (see page 74) and Dreimäderlhaus (Schreyvogelgasse 10) have fine examples of Biedermeier design; furniture is on display in the Museum for Applied Arts; and original pieces can still be found in antiques shops throughout the city, though they come with a hefty price tag.

(1897–1910). The neighbouring **Café Prückel** is a welcome sight if you need a break. The Stubenring passes near the **Postsparkasse** (Savings Bank), another masterpiece by Otto Wagner.

## OUTSIDE THE RING

The Innere Stadt and the Ringstrasse by no means have a monopoly on Vienna's sights. There's plenty more to be seen outside the Ring, from royal palaces to the Funeral Museum.

### HUNDERTWASSER HAUS

Dismissed by many as a bit of a joke, the whimsical **Hundertwasser Haus ⑲** is a hugely popular tourist attraction. This public housing complex in Kegelgasse was designed by Austria's best-known artist of recent times, Friedensreich Hundertwasser (1928–2000). The gently undulating facades of 52 apartments are decorated with bright paintwork, tiles, ceramics and onion domes. In the nearby Untere Weissgerberstrasse is Hundertwasser's own museum, the **Kunsthaus Wien** (daily 10am–6pm; tram 1, O: Radetzkyplatz; wheelchair access; www.kunsthauswien.com), which show both his work and changing exhibitions by his contemporaries.

*Hundertwasser Haus facade*

# BELVEDERE

The summer palace of Prince Eugene of Savoy is regarded as the finest flower of Vienna's baroque residential architecture. Though close to the Innere Stadt, in the 3rd District, the **Belvedere** ⓴ (Unteres Belvedere, daily 10am–6pm; Oberes Belvedere, daily 9am–6pm; tram D; www.belvedere.at) is an enchanted world apart with its allegorical sculptures, fountains, waterfalls and gardens.

## Incineration plant

Another of Friedensreich Hundertwasser's projects can be seen at the Fernwärmewerk at Spittelau (U-Bahn: Spittelau), an incinerator whose output is used to heat 60,000 homes. Decorated by the artist in a characteristically colourful way, it is crowned by a vast image of the artist's cap.

The **Unteres** (Lower) **Belvedere** was built by Johann Lukas von Hildebrandt in 1714–16, and served as Prince Eugene's summer residence. (His winter palace is another architectural gem, now brightening the lives of bureaucrats in the Finance Ministry on Himmelpfortgasse.) The palace was acquired by Maria Theresa after the prince's death, and was used by various members of the Habsburg dynasty, including Archduke Franz Ferdinand, whose assassination at Sarajevo in 1914 sparked off World War I. In 1955, the four victorious powers of World War II met in the Upper Belvedere to sign the treaty which confirmed Austria's independence as a neutral country.

The Lower Belvedere previously provided a home for the collection of baroque art, but this has now moved to the Oberes Belvedere and the space left is used for temporary exhibitions. Of the palace's exquisitely ornate interior the highlight is probably the highly adorned rococo gilt-and-mirrored Golden Cabinet. The palace's **Orangerie** (access through the Lower Belvedere) was previously the Museum of Medieval Art, but the permanent collection has for the most part, like the baroque works, moved to the Oberes Belvedere. The Orangerie is now used to share the exhibitions put on in the rest of the palace. Beside the Orangerie is the **Prunkstall** (10am–noon), part of the stables and now used to display some more of the extensive holdings of medieval art previously hidden in the museum's storerooms.

Prince Eugene held banquets and other festivities in the **Oberes** (Upper) **Belvedere**, completed in 1723. Today it houses a wide-ranging **collection** of Austrian art from the Middle Ages to the present day. The gallery reflects the Austro-Hungarian Empire's image as a declining world power, culminating in a final grand artistic fling around 1900. As well as the excellent collections of medieval and baroque art (the latter including works by

*Prince Eugene's summer palace, the Lower Belvedere (1716)*

The Kiss by Gustav Klimt

Franz Anton Maulbertsch and Martino Altomonte), there are fine examples of German Romanticism (including works by Caspar David Friedrich). However, the star exhibits for most people are from the collections of the *fin de siècle* and the Vienna Secession. These include such masterpieces as *The Kiss* by Gustav Klimt and Egon Schiele and Oskar Kokoschka are also well represented. However, Klimt's portrait of *Adele Bloch-Bauer* no longer hangs in the gallery, as it was handed back to the Jewish family it had belonged to before the war (it was appropriated by the Nazis and had ended up in the Belvedere collection). The small but stunning collection of Impressionist and post-Impressionist art features works by Monet, Renoir, Cézanne, Van Gogh and Munch, and sculptures by Rodin and Degas. The Upper Belvedere **terrace** offers a splendid view of the city skyline, remarkably little changed since Bellotto-Canaletto painted it in 1760. For your walk through the gardens, the best place to start is at the Oberes Belvedere. The sunset view is a pure delight.

## NEARBY MUSEUM

Close by in the Arsenal is the **Heeresgeschichtliches Museum** ❷❶ (Museum of Military History, daily 9am–5pm; www.hgm.or.at). Housed in the earliest purpose-built museum in the city, the beautifully displayed, and extensive, holdings of the museum give a fascinating insight into the history of the Austrian state. The displays on World War II are hard-hitting, particularly the news footage of Vienna. One interesting, if slightly morbid, item on display is the bloodstained tunic of Archduke Franz Ferdinand which can be found next to the car in which he was assassinated.

## ZENTRALFRIEDHOF

The Viennese, it must be said, do not consider it morbid to be interested in funerals and admire *eine schöne Leich* (a nice corpse). They enjoy a walk through the **Zentralfriedhof** (Central Cemetery; Simmeringer Hauptstrasse 234; daily Nov–Feb 8am–5pm, Mar, Oct 7am–6pm, Apr–Sept 7am–7pm; tram 7, 71) in the southern district of Simmering. Opened in 1874, the cemetery has 200 hectares (500 acres) of funerary monuments that pay homage to the city's greats: musicians such as Beethoven, Schubert, Brahms and Schönberg, and writers Arthur Schnitzel and Franz Werfel. A map of the cemetery is available at Tor (Gate) 2.

The cemetery boasts the morbidly unique **Bestattungsmuseum** (Funeral Museum; Mon–Fri 9am–4.30pm, Mar–Oct also Sat; tram 7, 71; www.bestattungsmuseum.at). At this typically Viennese institution you can find out about all sorts of curious items, including reusable coffins (after the ceremony, the hinged flaps would open, leaving the corpse behind while the coffin was taken off to be used again). The museum's ashtrays are inscribed *'Rauchen sichert Arbeitsplätze'* ('Smoking Guarantees Jobs').

## THE GASOMETERS

Also in Simmering are the **Gasometers** (U-Bahn 3: Gasometer). These four gasholders were built for the city in 1896–9. Following their decommissioning in 1986, a scheme was launched to give the gasometers a new lease of life. Today the complex features shops, restaurants, cafés and bars, a multi-screen cinema and a hall seating 4,200 people. It's also home to offices, flats, student accommodation and the Vienna National Archives.

## FURTHER SIGHTS

To the west of the Ringstrasse, leading out from the MuseumsQuartier (see page 53), is **Mariahilferstrasse**, the city's most popular shopping thoroughfare. Also, at No. 212, stands the **Technisches Museum**

*One of the city's gasometers*

(Technical Museum; Mon–Fri 9am–6pm, Sat–Sun 10am–6pm; tram 52, 60: Penzinger Strasse; www.technischesmuseum.at). The main hall has steam engines, a huge steel-making crucible while aeroplanes swoop down from above. There are wheels to turn and levers to pull, making this a boredom-beating place for children, and the clearly laid-out exhibits explain the science behind many of the machines in an exemplary fashion.

Just to the south, along the Linke Wienzeile, are the fruit, vegetable and meat stalls of the famous **Naschmarkt** ㉒ (food market), which has been here since the 16th century. Originally it was beside a river, the Wienfluss. In the 19th century the river was roofed over and stalls set up on the roof. Notice the decorated Jugendstil facade of **Majolikahaus** at No. 40, by Secessionist architect Otto Wagner. Nearby is the venerable **Theater an der Wien**, built in 1801 for the impresario Emanuel Schikaneder, the librettist of Mozart's *Magic Flute*.

The elaborate Majolikahaus

Further west is the **Haydnhaus** (Haydngasse 19; Tues–Sun 10am–1pm, 2pm–6pm; free entry on the first Sun of each month; U-Bahn 3: Zieglergasse; www.wienmuseum.at) where the composer lived from 1797 until his death on 31 May 1809. His two oratorios *The Creation* and *The Seasons* were conceived and written in this house.

Further west still, in the suburb of Penzing (14th District), is one of Otto Wagner's most important works, the **Kirche am Steinhof** (guided tour only; enquire at service@wienmuseum.at; U-Bahn 4 to Unter St Veit then bus 47A). This masterpiece of *Jugendstil* design is the church for the Vienna's enlightened psychiatric hospital.

North of the Innere Stadt, at Berggasse 19, is the **Freud Museum** ❷❸ (Wed–Mon 10am–6pm; tram D: Schlickgasse; www.freud-museum.at), dedicated to the father of psychoanalysis. Sigmund Freud lived here from 1891 until the arrival of the Nazis in 1938, when he fled to England. While most of his books and belongings are in London (including the couch), the waiting room has been faithfully reconstructed, with advice from his daughter Anna Freud. The entrance hall is particularly evocative, with his hat, walking stick and suitcase initialled SF. The rooms where he did his consulting now have a display on his life, while the rest of the apartment is given over to temporary exhibitions.

One fascinating room has home movie footage showing Freud during his final years.

Beyond the Freud Museum is the **Palais Liechtenstein** (the collection can only be viewed as part of guided tours held on selected Fridays and pre-booked events, check the website for details; tram D: Bauernfeldplatz; www.palaisliechtenstein.com), the garden palace of the princes of Liechtenstein. Now beautifully restored and showing off its wonderful frescoes, it holds an exceptionally fine collection of baroque paintings.

The **Schubert Geburtshaus** at Nussdorferstrasse 54 (Tues–Sun 10am–1pm, 2–6pm; free entry on the first Sun of each month; tram 37, 38: Canisiusgasse; www.wienmuseum.at) is a museum set in the house where the composer was born in 1797, and where he spent the first four and a half years of his life.

*Schönbrunn in summer*

# SCHÖNBRUNN

Affairs of the state were not something Maria Theresa shied away from, but she did prefer to handle them in the calmer setting of **Schönbrunn** ㉔ (daily Nov–Mar 8.30am–5pm, Apr–Oct 8.30am–5.30pm; U-Bahn 4: Schönbrunn; tram 10, 60: Schönbrunn; bus 10A: Schönbrunn; www.schoenbrunn.at). Almost as soon as she came to the throne in 1740, she moved into the palace, which Leopold I built as a summer residence and her father, Karl VI, had used as a shooting lodge. If the Hofburg is the oversized expression of a dynasty that outgrew itself, Schönbrunn is the smiling, serene expression of the personality of one woman, imperial nonetheless. Finding Fischer von Erlach's ideas for designing a 'super Versailles' too pompous, Maria Theresa brought in her favourite architect, Nikolaus Pacassi. He made Schönbrunn an imposing edifice, creating warm and decorative rococo interiors, which were a symbol of Maria Theresa's 'idyllic absolutism'.

*Sculpture at Schönbrunn*

## THE GARDENS

To appreciate Schönbrunn's tendency to pleasure rather than imperial pomp, visit the **gardens** first. With the exception of the Kammergarten (Chamber Garden) and Kronprinzengarten (Crown Prince Garden) immediately left and right of the palace, the park has always been open to the public as Maria Theresa seems to have liked having the Viennese people around her. The park, laid out in classical French manner, is dominated by the **Gloriette,** a magnificent colonnade perched on the crest of a hill. It is difficult to say which view is prettier – the graceful silhouette of the Gloriette against a sunset viewed from the palace, or a bright morning view from the Gloriette over the whole of Vienna to the north and the Wienerwald away to the south.

## Flash fittings

The most ornate room at Schönbrunn is known as the Millions Room, with walls panelled in costly rosewood in the rococo style. Gilt-edged cartouches set into wood contain Indian miniature paintings showing the court and private lives of the 16th and 17th-century Moghul emperors. To make them fit, original paintings were cut up by members of the imperial family and arranged as collages to form new pictures.

On the way to the Gloriette you will pass the Neptune Fountain and countless other statues of ancient mythology. East of the fountain are the half-buried artificial **'Roman ruins'**, a romantic folly built by JF Hetzendorf von Hohenberg in 1778, complete with fragmented Corinthian columns, friezes and archways. Nearby is the Schöner Brunnen, the 'beautiful spring' discovered by Emperor Matthias around 1615, from which the palace took its name, and which provided the water supply. West of Neptune is the **Tiergarten** (zoo; Jan, Oct–Dec 9am–4.30pm, Feb–Mar 9am–5pm, Apr–Sept 9am–6.30pm), established in 1752 by François of Lorraine, the consort of Maria Theresa. Not everyone enjoys seeing animals behind bars, but the aquarium, with its 'walk-through' flooded rainforest, is worth a visit. You can also lose yourself in

The Riesenrad at the Prater

the topiary **maze** and a **Tyrolean Garden**. Other attractions include the **Palmenhaus** (Palm House) and **Wüstenhaus** (Desert Experience House).

## THE PALACE

Crossing the courtyard to the palace's front entrance, you'll see on the right the **Schlosstheater**, now the site of summer chamber-opera performances.

A guided tour of the **palace** reveals something of the cosy ambience enjoyed by Maria Theresa and her successors: her breakfast room, decorated with the needlework of the empress and her myriad daughters; the **Spiegelsaal** (Hall of Mirrors), in which the young Mozart gave his first royal recital; the **Chinesisches Rundkabinett** (Chinese Round Room), also known as Maria Theresa's Konspirationstafelstube ('Top Secret Dining Room'). For her secret consultations, a table rose from the floor with a completely prepared dinner so that no servants would be present during the conversation. Guests used the **billiard room** while awaiting an audience with Franz Joseph. He, too, preferred Schönbrunn to the Hofburg and kept his mistress, actress Katharina Schratt, in a villa in the neighbouring district of Hietzing. Also on view is the bedroom where he died on 30 November 1916, at the age of 86.

The stately and the human are poignantly juxtaposed in the opulence of the ballrooms and dining rooms and the intimacy of the living quarters. The **Napoleon Room** (originally Maria Theresa's bedroom) was used by the French emperor on his way to victory at Austerlitz and by his son, the Duke of Reichstadt, in his final sad years. It is both pathetic and awesome to sense Napoleon's presence in a room that now contains his son's death mask and stuffed pet bird. Down the corridor, the last Habsburg (Karl I) abdicated at the end of World War I and Kennedy and Khrushchev met for dinner at the height of the Cold War. In the adjoining **Wagenburg Museum** (mid-Mar–Nov daily 9am–5pm, Dec–mid-Mar 10am–4pm; www.khm.at) you can see an impressive collection of coaches used by the imperial court, including the gilded coronation carriage of Holy Roman Emperor Karl VI.

## ACROSS THE DANUBE

### THE PRATER

Over the Aspernbrücke, cross the Donaukanal at the junction of Franz-Josefs-Kai and Stubenring to reach the island between the Donaukanal and the much wider main channel to the east. The southern part is occupied by the **Prater** ❷ (15 Mar–31 Oct daily approximately 11am–10pm; free; www.praterservice.at). This is Vienna's most extensive park, once reserved for the nobility but opened up

*The soaring Millennium Tower*

to the public in 1766 by Emperor Joseph II. In 2016 the Prater celebrated its 250th anniversary. Its most prominent feature is the old-fashioned amusement park with the famous **Riesenrad** ❷❻ (Ferris Wheel; usually open all day long, see website for exact opening times; www.wienerriesenrad.com) that was immortalised in the film *The Third Man*. Built in 1897, it is one of the oldest and largest Ferris wheels in the world, 65m (213ft) high, and provides sweeping views over the city. Next to the Riesenrad is the terminal of the **Liliput-Bahn** (Lilliput Railway; www.liliputbahn.com), which provides transport around the park (see website for schedule). New to the Prater in 2023, **Panorama Vienna** is a unique exhibition space that shows art in the form of giant 360-degree panoramas. The gigantic concrete structure represents the tradition of rotundas in the Prater.

*Vienna viewed from the vineyards of Kahlenberg*

## DONAUINSEL

You can reach the real Danube River (as opposed to the Danube Canal) along Lassallestrasse and over the Reichsbrücke. An artificial recreation island featuring beaches, barbecue picnic areas and sports facilities, the **Donauinsel** ㉗ runs 21km (13 miles) along the middle of the river. The 'Blue Danube' is actually yellowish-brown in colour due to the lime content of the riverbed. Continue on the Wagramerstrasse, past the attractive modern complex of buildings forming the **UNO-City** ㉘ (officially the Vienna International Centre; guided tours Mon–Fri 11am, 2pm, 3.30pm; bring your passport; www.unvienna.org) to the **Alte Donau** (the Old Danube). This self-contained arm of the river is closed off for sailing, fishing and bathing, and is actually blue. The banks are lined with beaches, marinas and well-pruned gardens.

The **Donaupark** links the old and new Danube; more tranquil than the Prater, it has been laid out with flowerbeds, an artificial lake and sports arenas. It also features the 252m (827ft) tall **Donauturm** (Danube Tower; www.donauturm.at), with fine views from its terrace. Back on the city side of the Danube, at Handelskai near the Nordbahnbrücke, is the **Millennium Tower** ㉙. At over 200m (656ft), this is the tallest enclosed building in Central Europe (www.millenniumtower.at).

## VIENNA'S SUBURBS

You should devote at least a day to exploring the 19th District of **Döbling**, the most gracious and elegant of Vienna's suburbs. Stretching from the Danube Canal to the slopes of the Wienerwald, Döbling includes Sievering, Grinzing, Heiligenstadt, Nussdorf and Kahlenberg. It is dotted with villas, parks, vineyards and, of course, the *Heuriger* wine gardens, which are especially popular in **Grinzing**.

Heiligenstadt and the other neighbourhoods of Döbling provide a vital clue to the secret of Vienna's charm. Vienna is not a conventional big city, but rather a collection of villages clustered around the Innere Stadt. These village-suburbs provide a convenient getaway from what the Viennese call the *Hektik* of metropolitan life.

Catch tram D in front of the Votivkirche at Schottentor (or take U-Bahn 4 to its terminus), and take it to **Heiligenstadt**, the heart of Vienna's 'Beethoven country'. Although opening times are restricted, you can then stop off at **Villa Wertheimstein** (Döblinger Hauptstrasse 96; Sat 3pm–5pm, Wed 9.30–11.30am; www.bezirksmuseum.at), a masterpiece of 19th-century Biedermeier architecture, full of period pieces, and featuring a lovely English garden.

At the end of the line (Heiligenstädter Park), walk across the park past the monument to Beethoven to Pfarrplatz 2, the prettiest of the composer's many Viennese homes. Take bus 38A to Probusgasse 6, the house where, in 1802, the composer penned his tragic *Heiligenstadt Testament*, in which he told his two brothers of his encroaching deafness. Today it is the **Beethoven Museum** (Tues–Sun 10am–1pm and 2–6pm; free entry on the first Sun of each month; www.wienmuseum.at).

## THE HOHENSTRASSE

To explore the hills and woods that lie to the north of the city, take the 38A bus from Heiligenstadt U-Bahn up to the **Höhenstrasse** leading to Kahlenberg and Leopoldsberg on the northern slopes of the Wienerwald. The route offers a grandiose view of the city and surrounding country. You'll find it difficult to believe that you're still inside the city limits. If time permits, get out at one of the stops en route and have a walk around.

Near the end of the Hohenstrasse is the **Kahlenberg**. Since the end of the 18th century, the heights of Kahlenberg have been dotted with fashionable summer homes offering what is known as *Sommerfrische* (cool summer respite from the city heat). During two steaming hot days in July 1809, the Viennese aristocracy had a grandstand view of Napoleon's Battle of Wagram against the Austrians. Sipping cool Nussdorfer white wine, they watched the slaughter of 40,000 Austrians and 34,000 Frenchmen on the other side of the Danube.

*Klosterneuburg abbey*

The Höhenstrasse goes as far as **Leopoldsberg**, the very edge of the Wienerwald and the extreme eastern point of the European Alps. On a clear day, you can see about 100km (60 miles) eastwards from the terrace of the **Leopoldskirche** to the Carpathian Mountains in Slovakia.

## KLOSTERNEUBURG

A short detour 7km (4 miles) to the north takes you to the imposing Augustine abbey of **Klosterneuburg** ㉚ (Mon–Fri 10am–6pm, Sat 10am–5pm, Sun noon–5pm; U-Bahn 4 to Heiligenstadt and then bus 400 or 402; www.stift-klosterneuburg.at). A story claims it was founded by Duke Leopold III of Babenberg in 1106 on the spot where his bride's lost veil was discovered by his hunting dogs. In fact, its foundation is earlier, but little of the original edifice remains. Karl VI, who was very much taken with Spain, undertook major alterations in the 18th century, making it a baroque version of El Escorial. He wanted a combined palace and church with nine domes, each topped with a crown of the House of Habsburg. Only two were completed in his lifetime: the crown of the empire on the big dome and of the Austrian archduchy on the little one. Klosterneuburg also features Austria's oldest winery, where an atmospheric and informative tour through the baroque cellars explores the 900-year history of wine production at the Augustine abbey. The tour is topped off with a wine tasting.

The baroque ornamentation is indeed impressive, but the whole trip is made worthwhile by the **Leopoldskapelle**, with its magnificent **Verdun Altar** of 1181 containing 45 enamelled panels depicting scenes from the Scriptures. It served as a graphic Bible for the

*The ruined 13th-century Burg Aggstein*

poor who could not read the stories.

# THE WIENERWALD

While it can be seen along the Höhenstrasse, to appreciate the **Wienerwald** properly, you must visit the villages hidden away in the forest to the south and southwest of Vienna (for information on local buses and trains check on www.wienerlinien.at). First head out to Perchtoldsdorf, a

## Escaping the city

The sights around Vienna, from the Wienerwald to further afield in Burgenland, are all easily reached as a day trip from the city, using Austria's excellent network of public transport. The train (see www.oebb.at) will get you to most places, and those sights without a station will be served by connecting buses (see www.postbus.at).

serene little village amid heather-covered hills, vineyards and fir trees. Continue south to Burg Liechtenstein, a 'ruined castle' built in 1873 on the site of the 12th-century home of the Liechtenstein dynasty. The park is an ideal spot for a picnic. In **Mödling** you can see the 15th-century Gothic Spitalkirche (Hospital Church) and the house (Hauptstrasse 79) where Beethoven worked on his *Missa Solemnis*.

To the west is **Hinterbrühl**. Romantics like to believe that the picturesque mill, Höldrichsmühle (converted into an inn), is where Franz Schubert wrote songs for the miller's daughter Rosi (*'Die schöne Müllerin'*) in 1823. In fact the story originated in an 1864 operetta devoted to the composer's life. But the inn's wines can make believers of us all.

Beyond is the Sattelbach Valley and the Cistercian abbey of **Heiligenkreuz** (Holy Cross), founded in 1133. Heiligenkreuz is named after the relic of a piece of the True Cross, given to Austria by the King of Jerusalem in the 12th century and kept in the tabernacle behind the high altar. The courtyard features a **Trinity Column** (Pillar of the Plague), the work of baroque artist Giovanni Giuliani, who also designed the basilica's splendid choir stalls. The structure retains its Romanesque western facade. Along its south side is a graceful 13th-century cloister with 300 red columns.

In the town **churchyard** you'll find a tomb bearing the inscription: *'Wie eine Blume sprosst der Mensch auf und wird gebrochen'* ('Like a flower, the human being unfolds – and is broken'). This is the grave of Baroness Mary Vetsera, the 17-year-old who died in 1889 at nearby **Mayerling** in an apparent suicide pact with her lover Crown Prince Rudolf, heir to the Austro-Hungarian Empire. To hush the scandalmongers, the hunting lodge where the Mayerling tragedy occurred was demolished shortly thereafter and replaced with a Carmelite convent.

# BADEN

From town the Badner Bahn (www.wlb.at) will take you from the Kärntner Ring to the romantic Helenental Valley and the spa of **Baden bei Wien**, 25km (16 miles) south of Vienna, which became a Unesco World Heritage site in 2021. Baden's supposedly medicinal springs were enjoyed as far back as Roman times, but were made fashionable by Franz I in 1803 when Baden became the very symbol of upright Viennese Biedermeier prosperity. The gentry of Vienna built their summer villas here in an architectural style that the town is now famous for, and bathed in the gorgeous 36°C (97°F) sulphurous waters. The thermal waters can still be enjoyed in the indoor pool (Brusattiplatz 4), open-air pools (Helenen Strasse 19–21) and mineral-water pools (Römerplatz 1). Return via **Gumpoldskirchen**, a village with first-rate *Heuriger* wine gardens and not a bad place to stay if you want to be out of town (see page 139).

# THE DANUBE VALLEY

If your visit gives you time for only one side-trip it should unquestionably be along the **Danube Valley** ③, in particular the magical area known as the Wachau between the historic towns of Melk and Krems. About an hour west of Vienna, this is where the Danube Valley is at its most scenic, by turns both charming and verdant with vineyards, apricot orchards and rustic villages, then suddenly forbidding with ruined medieval castles and rocky cliffs half hidden in mist. This is a landscape whose atmosphere is heavy with myth. Legend has it that the Burgundy kings of the medieval German epic, the *Nibelungenlied*, passed this spot en route to the kingdom of the Huns. The crusaders also passed through here on their way to the Holy Land. Take a Danube River cruise if you simply want to sit and dream as this mythical world passes you by. For a closer look at the towns and castles on the way it's best to travel by train or bus.

## MELK

On a leisurely tour of the Danube Valley, 84km (52 miles) by the Westautobahn from Vienna, the Benedictine abbey of **Melk** ③ (Stift Melk; daily Apr–Oct 9am–5.30pm, Nov–Mar Sat–Sun 10am–4.30pm, Mon–Fri pre-booked guided tours only; www.stiftmelk.at) makes an ideal starting

*The abbey of Melk*

point. Towering high above the river on a protruding rock, this is one of the region's most majestic sights. Its position overlooking a bend in the river made this a strategic site from the time of the Romans. The Babenberg predecessors of the Habsburgs erected a fortress here in the 10th century, which they handed over to the Benedictines in 1106. The monks gradually created an abbey of huge proportions, enhanced by the baroque transformations of architect Jakob Prandtauer in 1702. Two towers, together with the octagonal dome and the lower Bibliothek (Library) and Marmorsaal (Marble Hall), form a harmonious group. The interior of the church is rich in reds and golds with a high altar by Antonio Beduzzi and superbly sculpted pulpit, choir and confessionals. The ceiling frescoes are by Johann Michael Rottmayr, whose work also adorns Vienna's Karlskirche.

Before crossing the Danube, make a quick detour to the village of **Mauer**, 10km (6 miles) due east of Melk, to see the late Gothic wooden altarpiece in the parish church. The work, by an anonymous local artist around 1515, depicts the Adoration of the Virgin Mary with a wealth of vivid detail.

## MEDIEVAL TOWNS OF THE WACHAU

The Wachauer Strasse, along the north bank, is dotted with apricot orchards and vineyards, old *Weinhüterhütten* (vineguards' huts) and villages with *Heuriger* wine gardens.

On the opposite bank, you can see Schönbühel and the 13th-century ruins of **Burg Aggstein**. The castle was once owned by a robber baron named Jörg Scheck vom Wald, popularly known as 'Schreckenwald' (Terror of the Forest). One of his favourite activities was to lead prisoners to his rose garden, on the edge of a sheer precipice, where they were given the choice of either starving to death or ending it quickly by jumping 53m (175ft) onto the rocks below.

Back on the happier north bank, visit the town of **Spitz**, with its late Gothic **St Mauritius** church. It's known for its statues of the Apostles in the 1380 organ gallery, and the baroque painting of the Martyrdom of St Mauritius by Kremser (Martin Johann) Schmidt. In the village of **St Michael**, look for seven stone hares perched on the roof of the 16th-century church. These commemorate a particularly vicious winter when snowdrifts were said to have enabled the animals to jump clear over the church. In the village of **Weissenkirchen** is a fortified church, which was originally surrounded by four towers, a moat, ramparts and 44 cannons.

The most romantic of these medieval towns is **Dürnstein**, famous as the site of Richard the Lion Heart's imprisonment in 1192–3. Devastated by the Swedish army in 1645, the castle of

*Romantic Dürnstein*

Kuenringer is more interesting to look at from below than it is to visit. But do make a point of seeing Dürnstein's **abbey church**, a baroque structure with a splendid carved wooden door to the abbey courtyard and an imposing statue of the resurrected Christ at the church entrance.

## KREMS

**Krems** ❸ is the heart of the region's wine industry and historically one of the Danube Valley's most important trading centres. Today, you can enjoy its superb Gothic, Renaissance and baroque residences on tranquil, tree-shaded squares. Start on Südtiroler Platz and walk through the 15th-century Steiner Tor (Town Gate) with its Gothic pepper-pot towers. Turn left up Schmidgasse to Körnermarkt and the Dominikanerkirche (Dominican Church), transformed into an important museum

### A SONG FOR RICHARD

During the Crusade of 1191, the brave but cheeky English king, Richard the Lionheart, enraged Leopold V von Babenberg by replacing the Austrian flag in Acre, Palestine, with the English one. Worse than that, he prevented the Austrians from sharing in the booty. But, on his way home, though dressed as a peasant, Richard was recognised and thrown into the darkest dungeon of Dürnstein Castle. He languished there for several years until the faithful minstrel Blondel came looking for him, singing a song known only to the king and himself. Richard revealed his place of imprisonment by joining in the chorus. His ransom, 23,000kg (22.6 tons) of silver, was enough to finance the Holy Roman Empire's expedition to Sicily and to build a new Ring Wall around Vienna.

*Prosperous Krems*

of medieval art. Continue round to Pfarrplatz, dominated by the **Pfarrkirche**, a lovely church remodelled (1616–30) by two Italian architects and decorated with altar paintings by Franz Anton Maulbertsch and the masterful frescoes of Kremser Schmidt. The oldest square in Krems, Hoher Markt, features a masterpiece of Gothic residential architecture, the arcaded **Gozzoburg**, built around 1270. Take a stroll along the Untere Landstrasse to see some elegant baroque facades and the fine Renaissance **Rathaus** (Town Hall). On a contemporary note, a modern art museum has opened in the town, the **Kunsthalle Krems** (www.kunsthalle.at) and close by a **Karikaturmuseum** (www.karikaturmuseum.at). It includes work by the Austrian cartoonist Manfred Deix, who was renowned for being less than flattering to his fellow-countrymen.

Before leaving Krems, try some of the local 'new wine' served in one of the leafy courtyards along the Obere Landstrasse.

## TO THE EAST

Heading east from Vienna along the Danube traces the ancient eastern European boundary of the Roman Empire. About 36km (22 miles) from the city, at Petronell, are the remains of **Carnuntum** (www.carnuntum.at), which was once the capital of the Roman province of Pannonia (embracing much of modern Hungary and eastern Austria). In the 2nd century AD, under Hadrian and Marcus Aurelius, it was a thriving commercial centre. Various festivals are held throughout the site over the summer months.

Five kilometres (3 miles) south of Petronell is **Rohrau**, a pretty but small village that is famous for being the birthplace of Joseph Haydn. You can visit the beautifully restored thatched farmhouse

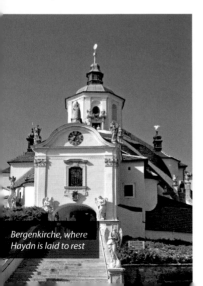

*Bergenkirche, where Haydn is laid to rest*

where the classical composer was born in 1732. Concerts are held here during spring and summer. Nearby is the Schloss Rohrau, the baroque castle of the Harrach family, who were early patrons of young Haydn and lived here until 1945. After they moved out, the building was renovated and opened to the public; it now houses a fine collection of 17th-century Spanish, Flemish and Italian art, and beautiful gardens that make for a very relaxing wander in nice weather.

# NEUSIEDLERSEE

Beyond Rohrau, and further east, is the **Neusiedler See** ③④ (www.
neusiedlersee.com). This birdwatchers' paradise teems with heron,
teal, waterfowl, wild geese and egret. The water of the lake is so
shallow that it's possible to wade right across – only a few spots
are more than 1.5m (5ft) deep. If you do cross, be aware that the
southern end of the lake belongs to Hungary and you may need
your passport, which presents a slight conundrum to swimmers,
waders and paddlers without adequate means of carrying important documents. Flat-bottomed boats can be hired for fishing and
in winter you can go skating and ice-sailing. Along the lake's western shores are the villages of **Rust** and **Mörbisch**, both famous for
the storks that use local chimneys for nesting. Mörbisch, on the
Hungarian border, is particularly attractive, and the wine gardens
are simply marvellous.

# EISENSTADT

The baroque town of **Eisenstadt** ③⑤, 52km (32 miles) south of
Vienna, is where Joseph Haydn worked from 1761 as musical
director for the Hungarian prince Paul Esterházy. His house, the
**Haydn-Haus** (www.haydnhaus.at), contains his collection of
paintings, sheets of music and personal possessions. Haydn loved
Eisenstadt and wanted to live and die here. He managed the living,
but died in Vienna, without having taken the precaution of specify-
ing where he wanted to be buried. Unfortunately, shortly after he
was buried in Vienna in 1809, someone stole his skull, which was
put on exhibition. The headless body was eventually returned to
Eisenstadt where the skull rejoined it in 1954; both now lie reu-
nited in a white marble grave at the **Bergenkirche**. The church is
also noted for a Kalvarienberg, a Calvary display of life-size figures
showing the stations of the cross, displayed in a series of austere
dungeon-like rooms.

*Strauss statue in the Stadtpark*

# THINGS TO DO

## ENTERTAINMENT

### OPERA

It's difficult to think of a cultural institution in another European capital that holds the privileged place of the **Staatsoper** (National Opera; www.wiener-staatsoper.at) in Vienna. Since this is Austria, even those who loathe opera can be tempted in and converted. A Mozart performance is always a classic; while the more well-rounded opera-goers might take on Wagner or Alban Berg.

If you have tickets for a première or other gala performance, you should wear evening dress, though even on an ordinary night, people turn up in black tie or long dress. Jeans and shorts are a definite no-no.

First-rate opera and operetta can also be heard at the **Volksoper** (Währingerstrasse 78; www.volksoper.at), and opera and ballet at the **Theater an der Wien** (Linke Wienzeile 6; www.theater-wien.at).

### MUSIC

Music is an integral part of Vienna. There really is something for everyone, with concerts held in historic buildings, including Schönbrunn and the Belvedere. However, the really serious music-making takes place in the city's famous concert halls, chief amongst them the **Musikverein** (Dumbastrasse 3; www.musikverein.at), now with four halls. The other major concert hall is the **Konzerthaus** (Lothringerstrasse 20; www.konzerthaus.at).

Festivals take place throughout the year, the most important being the **Wiener Festwochen** (www.festwochen.at) in May and June. The festivals and concert seasons are showcases for the city's ensembles, including the **Wiener Philharmoniker** (www.wienerphilharmoniker.at), one of the world's finest orchestras. Other fine orchestras resident in the city include the **Wiener Symphoniker** (www.wienersymphoniker.at), and the **Radio Symphonie Orchester Wien** (www.rso.orf.at). **Klang Forum Wien** (www.klangforum.at) specialises in contemporary music, while the **Concentus Musicus Wien** is one of Europe's most important early-music ensembles.

Of course, there are many opportunities to hear the music of composers associated with the city. In fact, the music of Mozart, Haydn, Schubert and Beethoven is performed in Vienna's oldest concert hall, the **Sala Terrena** (Singerstrasse 7; www.mozarthaus.at). You should also try to hear the celebrated **Wiener Sängerknaben** (Vienna Boys' Choir, www.wienersaengerknaben.at), who sing at Sunday Mass and other festivities in the Burgkapelle in the Hofburg.

## THEATRE

The **Burgtheater** (National Theatre; Dr Karl Lueger-Ring 2; www.burgtheater.at) is not just Vienna's proudest theatre, but also one of the leading ensembles of the German-speaking world. The related **Akademietheater** (Lisztrasse 1) focuses on modern and avant-garde drama.

*Performance in the Musikverein*

Performances are held all year round at Vienna's **English Theatre** at Josefsgasse 12 (www.englishtheatre.at). There are several English-speaking theatre groups in the city, and special performances are staged for children. Not far from here is the excellent **Josefstadt Theater** (Josefstädter Strasse 26; www.josefstadt.org) that always has interesting productions.

> ### Listings
>
> Music, film, theatre and nightlife options are endless in Vienna, so consult a copy of *Falter* (www.falter.at), the weekly listings magazine, for the latest information.

## CINEMA

Austrian cinema has a long history, stretching back to the early years of silent film. Vienna itself has some excellent cinemas, including the **Filmmuseum** (www.filmmuseum.at), underneath the Albertina, that puts on screenings of classic European and English-language films. The **Burg Kino** on the Ringstrasse (www.burgkino.at) shows original-language English movies, as well as regular screenings of *The Third Man* (see website for times).

Elsewhere, the **Urania Kino** in the observatory at the end of the Stubenring (Uraniastrasse 1) has a nice auditorium, while the **Künstlerhaus Kino** (www.k-haus.at) on Karlsplatz is the place to catch avant-garde and art-house films, as well as being the venue for a number of film festivals.

## NIGHTLIFE

The city is said to have more than 6,000 bars, nightclubs, discos and cabarets – with many of the most popular bars staying open round the clock. There are a few large clubs, but also many small venues with music provided by well-known DJs. There are cool lounge clubs, too, where people chill out to easy-listening sounds.

North of Stephansdom, the area around Ruprechtsplatz, Seitenstettengasse and Rabensteig forms the previously hot **Bermudadreieck** (Bermuda Triangle). Apart from the excellent **First Floor** bar (Seitenstettengasse 5; www.firstfloorbar.at), this area is now passé, and much of the action has passed on to the district around Naschmarkt and the railway arches along the **Hernalser Gürtel** (on the western edge of the 8th District). The district around **Bäckerstrasse** is also chic. The tacky nightclubs around **Kärntnerstrasse** cater largely to the tourist trade.

Over on the Donaukanal is one of Vienna's best-known clubs, **Flex** (www.flex.at), with a legendary sound system and top DJs as well as live bands. Other popular places include the cult Roxy (www.roxyclub.org) near Naschmarkt, where soul, funk, R'n'B and hip-hop grooves fill a basement space; and, in the 12th District, **U4** (www.u-4.at), a

*Night lights at the Donaukanal*

long-standing club and live music venue. Along the Gürtel the scene revolves around chic bars with DJs and some live music. Good places to check out include **Chelsea** (www.chelsea.co.at), occupying a converted railway arch and known for its pulsating live music; the hard-core electronic venue of **rhiz** (www.rhiz.wien); and **B72** (www.b72.at), where guitar music meets electronic beats and breaks to create a good sound.

# SHOPPING

Perhaps surprisingly, Vienna has a lot to offer for those keen to go shopping. Behind many of the city's grand façades – or at least those spaces that have not been snapped up by international chains – are quirky boutiques, elegant design shops or long-standing purveyors of luxury handmade goods, from shoes and *Tracht*, to cakes and pastries.

## WHERE AND WHEN TO SHOP

The winding streets of Vienna's **Inner City** are a good place to start any shopping expedition. Although now increasingly dominated by international names, especially along **Graben**, **Kohlmarkt** and **Kärntnerstrasse**, there are still numerous interesting local places to ferret out. To the west of the Inner City, **Mariahilferstrasse** is the other main shopping area: a long series of shops that only peters out at the Westbahnhof. Other good shopping districts can be found in the **university district** (near the Votivkirche) and around **Siebensterngasse** and **Lindengasse** in Neubau (the 7th District). Shops tend to be open between 9am and 6pm on weekdays, closing at 5pm on Saturday. Most places remain shut on Sundays.

## WHAT TO BUY

For general fashion a good place to start is **Steffl**, a large department store (Kärntnerstrasse 19; www.steffl-vienna.at) with a large number of concessions for both well-established and younger designers. Otherwise have a wander through the **Ringstrassen Galerien** nearby on the Kärtner Ring. In the 1st District most of the big-name designers can be found around Kohlmarkt, especially in the Goldenes Quartier, an extension of the elegant Kohlmarkt. The elegant Swiss watch company Chopard (www.chopard.com) has set up right at the start of the pedestrian zone. For some retail history visit the long-standing Austrian hat-makers Mühlbauer (Seilergasse 10; www.muehlbauer.at). Further afield check out the boutiques on Lindengasse and for up-and-coming Austrian designers do not miss **PARK** on Mondscheingasse (No. 20; www.park-onlinestore.com) close by.

For beautifully made *Tracht* (traditional Austrian clothing still popular in Vienna), go to **Tostmann Trachten** (Schottengasse 31; www.tostmann.at) or **Loden-Plankl** (Michaelerplatz 6; www.loden-plankl.at).

*Dried fruit at the Naschmarkt*

Vienna can also boast two world-class shoemakers. Neither **Rudolf Scheer** (Bräunerstrasse 4; www.scheer.at) or **Ludwig Reiter** (Mölkersteig 1; www.ludwigreiter.com) are cheap but their shoes are superbly crafted.

Classic Viennese designs are other items worth seeking out. For glass and porcelain, head to **Augarten** (Spiegelgasse 3; www.augarten.com) and **Lobmeyr** (Kärntnerstrasse 26; www.lobmeyr.at). Backhausen textiles can be found at **Österreichische**

**Werkstätten** (Kärntnerstrasse 6/4) who also have a museum of original works in the basement of the shop. For replicas of classic lamps and lighting, check out **Woka** (Palais Breuner, Singerstrasse 16).

As such an important centre for classical music, Vienna has a couple of excellent places to buy CDs and sheet music. **Gramola** (Graben 16) is the best place to find recordings, while **Doblinger** (Dorotheergasse 10) has a vast selection of scores.

*Christmas market at the Rathaus*

For food and drink, head for the city's best market on **Naschmarkt** or the wonderful selection at **Julius Meinl** (Graben 19). Seasonal specialities can be found in the many Christmas markets that take place in Vienna but the one outside the Rathaus is particularly rewarding. Wonderful patisserie can be found at confectioners such as **Demel** (Kohlmarkt 14; www.demel.com) and **Gerstner** (Kärntnerstrasse 51; www.gerstner-konditorei.at), while since 1840 six generations of the same family have been producing fine pastries and cakes at **L. Heiner** (Kärntnerstrasse 21).

## ACTIVE PURSUITS

The easiest way to get rid of excess *strudel* is by going for a walk or run in one of the city's many **parks**. The largest of these is the Prater, but there are parks dotted all around the Ringstrasse that give you a chance to stretch your legs.

**Cycling** is an enjoyable way of getting around Vienna – and of escaping traffic snarls. In 2022, **WienMobil** was launched as a bike sharing rental system with some 3,000 bikes available at over 200 stations around the clock. There is an app that supports the scheme and payment can be made using debit/credit card. Bicycles, mountain bikes and e-bikes can also be rented at a host of other outlets around the city. The Tourist Information Office website (www.wien.info/en/lifestyle-scene/sports/cycling) has comprehensive information about the WienMobil scheme, lists bicycle hire firms, cycling tours, and also provides regional maps of cycling routes.

See Vienna's spectacular hinterland by **hiking** along the well-marked paths of the Wienerwald. In the winter, these paths can be used for **cross-country skiing**.

The 21km (13-mile) beach of the Donauinsel provides outdoor **swimming**, along with facilities for **water skiing** and **windsurfing**. Döbling's **Krapfenwaldlbad** is a fashionable outdoor swimming pool, complete with a restaurant. Most handsome of the indoor swimming pools is the **Amalienbad**, Reumannplatz 23, with *Jugendstil* decor and an old-fashioned steam bath and sauna.

**Ice-skating** carries on year-round in the Wiener Stadthalle, Vogelweidplatz 14, and during the winter in Rathausplatz outside the town hall.

*Kids at Schönbrunn*

You can see professional football at Austria's national stadium in the Prater, or go to a match between the city's Bundesliga (first division) teams, Austria Vienna and SK Rapid.

## Youth centre

For information about events and activities for young people (aged 13 to 26), contact Jugendinfo at Babenbergerstrasse 1 (Mon–Fri 2.30–6.30pm; tel: 01-4000-84 100; www.wienxtra.at/jugendinfo).

# CHILDREN'S VIENNA

Vienna is a good destination for children. **Schönbrunn** (see page 68) has a number of distractions: there is the **Marionette Theatre** (www.marionettentheater.at) and maze, and children's museum (www.kindermuseumschoenbrunn.at) on the ground floor (west wing) of the palace. There's also a **zoo** at Schönbrunn and an **aquarium, Haus der Meeres** (www.haus-des-meeres.at), at Esterhazy Park. Also try the **Butterfly House** at Burggarten, and, for those who like stars, the city's **Planetarium** (Oswald Thomas Platz; www.planetarium-wien.at). Outside the city, on the eastern slopes of the Wienerwald, the **Lainz Wildlife Park** (www.lainzer-tiergarten.at) offers a visitor centre, forest playgrounds, nature trails and even close-up encounters with wild boar.

The **ZOOM Kindermuseum** (www.kindermuseum.at) is specifically for children, while the Museum of Modern Art (MOMOK), Museum of Fine Arts and Museum of Natural History all have children's programmes, and the Technical Museum and the House of Music both have lots to discover.

The **Prater funfair**, the **Spanish Riding School** (see page 44) and the view from the **Donauturm** (see page 73) are all must-sees and sure to captivate children. Playgrounds and beaches can be found on **Danube Island**. In summer, the **boats** on the Danube sometimes have children's events (www.ddsg-blue-danube.at).

# CALENDAR OF EVENTS

For information and ticket details, contact the Tourist Information Office, tel: 01-24555, or consult www.wien.info.

**January** Vienna Philharmonic's traditional *Neujahrskonzert* (New Year's Day concert), 11.15am at Musikverein; the *Ball der Philharmoniker* (Philharmonic Ball), at Musikverein, rivals the *Opernball* for prestige.

**February/March** *Opernball* (Opera Ball), at Staatsoper, the social event of the year; *Fasching* (Carnival) procession in Döbling.

**April** *Ostermarkt* (Easter Market): a country-fair atmosphere on Freyung in Innere Stadt; *Wiener Sängerknaben* (Vienna Boys' Choir) weekly Mass in the Hofburg's Burgkapelle; *OsterKlang Wien* (Vienna's Sounds of Easter) music festival; Vienna Marathon accompanied by popular festivities.

**May** Traditional May Day celebrations at Prater amusement park; the Condordia Ball in the sumptuous Vienna City Hall attracts local celebrities.

**June** *Wiener Festwochen* (Vienna Festival), featuring music, dance and theatrical productions at Theater an der Wien and Messepalast; Regenbogen (Rainbow) Parade on Ringstrasse; *Donaueninselfest* (Danube Island Festival), with funfair festivities; Donauinsel pop music festival, a free weekend event.

**July/August** SCL Youth Music Festival, presents young talent from around the world to perform a the Musikverein and Wiener Konzerthaus; jazz, rock, reggae and hip-hop music festivals at Wiesen, south of Vienna; Popfest Wien, current and diverse domestic pop with more than 50 acts on and around Karlsplatz.

**September** In-line Skating Marathon on the Ringstrasse.

**October** Viennale Film Festival; *Wean Hean* folk festival.

**November/December** *Christkindlmarkt* (Christmas Market) at Rathausplatz, Schönbrunn, Freyung, Spittelberg: carols, roast chestnuts, *Glühwein* and stalls laden with gifts; MuseumsQuartier courtyard decked with lights and decorations; concerts, recitals throughout the Innere Stadt; New Year's Eve *Hofburg Silvester Ball at the Imperial Palace*.

# FOOD AND DRINK

When it comes to Viennese cuisine, it is worth bearing in mind that this city was once the centre of the old Habsburg Empire of 60 million Eastern and Southern Europeans. The emperor and his archdukes and generals have gone, but not the Bohemian dumplings, the Hungarian goulash, the Polish stuffed cabbage and Serbian *schaschlik*, nor the plum, cherry and apricot brandies that accompany the Turkish coffee. And all are now frequently served with the lighter touch of the New Viennese Cuisine.

Dining out has always been a popular pastime in Vienna. It is part of Austrian culture to take the family out for lunch at the weekend and to meet friends in a *Beisl* (convivial Viennese equivalent of the bistro) or at the *Heuriger* wine garden. In restaurants, the emphasis is on good company, good wine, robust portions and, usually, reasonable prices for the quality of the ingredients – a dramatically different approach from many other European capitals.

When choosing a restaurant, something to bear in mind during the summer months is whether you can sit outside in a garden or *Schanigarten* (tables on the pavement with sunshades). If you're simply

Drinking coffee on Mariahilferstrasse

A Wurststand (sausage stand) in the city

after a quick snack, then look for a traditional *Würstelstand*, a small kiosk selling sausages and other local specialities, such as *Leberkäsesemmel* (liver pâté sandwich). These kiosks are open almost all day and are to be found on street corners all over the city.

## VIENNESE FARE

Two Viennese staples that you're likely to come across immediately are the *Wienerschnitzel* and the *Backhendl*. The *Wienerschnitzel* is a large, thinly sliced cutlet of veal crisply sautéed in a coating of flour, egg and seasoned breadcrumbs. *Backhendl* is roast chicken prepared in the same way. Viennese gourmets insist that the *Wienerschnitzel* be served with cold potato or cucumber salad. You should also make sure that it is a cut of veal *(vom Kalb)* and not pork *(vom Schwein)*, as in some of the cheaper establishments. The *Backhendl* is sometimes served with *Geröstete* (sautéed potatoes).

*Tafelspitz* (boiled beef) was Emperor Franz Joseph's favourite dish, and to this day is a form of ambrosia to the Viennese. Spice it up with *Kren* (horseradish) and *Schnittlauchsauce* (chive sauce). Another delight, originally from Hungary, is goulash – beef chunks stewed with onion, garlic, paprika, tomatoes and celery. *Debreziner* sausages, *Köménymagleves Nokedival* (caraway-seed soup with dumplings) and apple soup are three more Hungarian specialities.

From the Czech Republic comes Prague ham and *sauerkraut* soup; from Polish Galicia, roast goose; and from Serbia, peppery barbecued *cevapcici* meatballs and *schaschlik* brochettes of lamb with onions and green and red peppers.

Dumplings *(Knödel),* made from flour, yeast or potatoes, are an Austrian staple. The *Marillenknödel* is a dessert dumpling, made of potato with a piping hot apricot inside. Another delicious dessert dumpling is the *Topfenknödel,* made with a cream-cheese filling.

Hot desserts are, in fact, a speciality, and you should also try *Buchteln* or *Wuchteln*, yeast buns often filled with plum jam, and from Hungary the *Palatschinken*, pancakes filled with jam or nuts.

## VIENNESE SAUSAGE STANDS

They all go for it: society ladies in posh frocks, night owls, opera buffs, workers – they all stand together at the Sausage Stand. Typical fare includes frankfurters (usual hot dog sausage), *Debreziner* (thin and spicy), *Bratwurst* (hunky thick fried sausage) and *Kasekrainer* (thick and made with meat and cheese). *Burenwurst* is a sort of boiled *Bratwurst*. There are stands all over town, including: **Albertina Wurstelstand**, Augustinerplatz, 8am–midnight; **Hoher Markt** (the most famous), Marc Aurel Strasse, 9am–4am; and **Zur Oper**, Kärntnerstrasse, 10am–5am.

And don't forget the *Apfelstrudel*, a flaky pastry filled with thinly sliced apples, raisins and cinnamon.

Finally, there's one of the most famous and sinfully delicious chocolate cakes in the world, the *Sachertorte*. Join in the endless debate over whether or not it should be split into two layers and where the apricot jam should go.

### Wines and Wine Gardens

Wine in Vienna is almost always white, which the Viennese drink with meat and fish alike. The best known of Austrian white wines, the *Gumpoldskirchner*, has the full body and bouquet of its southern vineyards. The Viennese give equal favour to their own *Grinzinger, Nussdorfer, Sieveringer* and *Neustifter*. From the Danube Valley, with an extra natural sparkle, come the *Kremser, Dürnsteiner* and *Langenloiser*.

*Waitress service at Café Demel*

Of the reds, the *Vöslauer*, produced in Bad Vöslau near Baden, and the *Kalterersee*, imported from South Tyrol (Italy's Alto Adige region), are about the best. *Blaufränkisch* and *Zweigelt* are also reliable standbys.

To enjoy these wines in their original state, they should be ordered *herb* (dry). Often the producers will sweeten them for the foreign palate unless you specify otherwise. Perhaps the most pleasant thing about Viennese wine is the way in which it is drunk.

*A Viennese vineyard*

The Viennese have created a splendid institution, the *Heuriger*, where you can sip white wine on mild evenings under the stars. Winemakers are allowed by law to sell a certain amount of their new wine (also called *Heuriger*) directly to the public. They announce the new wine by hanging out a sprig of pine over the door and a sign saying *Ausg'steckt* (open). The *Heuriger* of **Grinzing** are extremely popular, but many of the best ones are out in **Nussdorf**, **Ober-Sievering** and **Neustift**. *Heuriger* gardens are generally open from mid-afternoon until late in the evening and at weekends for lunch (but it's better to check in advance).

The local *Gösser* beer presents a fair challenge to the powerful *Pilsner Urquell* imported from the Czech Republic. Among the brandies you should try the Hungarian *Barack* (apricot) and Serbian *Slivovitz* (plum).

## Coffee and the Kaffeehaus

The varieties of coffee in Vienna are virtually endless, and there are names for every shade from black to white. Ask for *einen kleinen Mokka* and you'll get a small, strong black coffee and stamp yourself as someone of French or Italian taste. A *Kapuziner*, topped with generous dollops of cream, is more Viennese; *ein Brauner*, with just a dash of milk, is as Viennese as can be. *Eine Melange* (pronounced 'melanksch'), a mixture of milk and coffee, is designed for sensitive stomachs; *ein Einspänner*, with whipped cream in a tall glass, is for aunts on Sundays; *ein Türkischer*, prepared semi-sweet in a copper pot, is for addicts of the Balkan Connection.

The Viennese *Kaffeehaus* dates back to the 17th century when, depending on which legend you choose, either a Polish spy named Kulczycki or a Greek merchant named Theodat opened the first café with a stock of coffee beans captured from the Turks. By the time of Maria Theresa the town was full of coffee houses, fashionable and shady, where gentry and intellectuals mingled. Some developed their own particular clientele – writers, artists, politicians – while the most prominent (Griensteidl, Café Central, Herrenhof) attracted all types.

*The latest news in a Vienna café*

*Delicious Sachertorte*

After a post-war lull, the institution made a grand comeback. In the Innere Stadt, the renovated **Café Central** is thriving once again. With chandeliers adorning the ceiling, the former imperial bakery **Café Demel** on the Kohlmarkt is said to have the best cakes in town. **Café Hawelka**, at Dorotheergasse 6, once popular with artists and antiques dealers, has become a hangout for the younger crowd. Artists now prefer **Alt-Wien**, at Bäckerstrasse 9, and the **Kleines Café**, Franziskanerplatz 3, with its superb interior design by architect Hermann Czech. Intellectuals have followed the example of the late Thomas Bernhard in favouring **Café Bräunerhof**, at Stallburggasse 2. This café is also popular with music-lovers for its Sunday afternoon chamber-music recitals. In the 6th District, **Café Sperl**, Gumpendorfer Strasse 11, is an elegant 100-year-old establishment complete with marble tables, *Jugendstil* chairs and an endless row of newspapers (including *The Times*, *Le Monde* and *La Stampa*).

## TO HELP YOU ORDER...

Waiter, waitress, please! **Bedienung, bitte!**
Could we have a table? **Wir hätten gerne einen Tisch.**
May I see the menu, please? **Die Speisekarte, bitte.**
The bill please. **Zahlen bitte.**
I would like… **Ich möchte gerne…**

Beer **ein Bier**
Bread **Brot**
Butter **Butter**
Cheese **Käse**
Dessert **Nachtisch**
Fish **Fisch**
Fruit **Obst**
Fruit juice **Fruchtsaft**
Ice cream **Eis**
Meat **Fleisch**

Menu **Speisekarte**
Milk **Milch**
Mineral water
　　**Mineralwasser**
Potatoes **Erdäpfel**
Salad **Salat**
Soup **Suppe**
Sugar **Zucker**
Tea **Tee**
Wine **Wein**

## ...AND READ THE MENU

**Auflauf** casserole
**Backhendl** sautéed chicken
**Debreziner** spicy sausage
**Ente** duck
**Erdbeeren** strawberries
**Faschiertes** minced meat
**Frittaten suppe** broth with
　　sliced crêpes
**Guglhupf** coffee cake
**Gurke** gherkin
**Kaiser-fleisch** cured pork
　　spare ribs
**Kaiser schmarrn** pancake
　　with fruit compote

**Kalb** veal
**Kirschen** cherries
**Knödeln** dumplings
**Kuchen** cake
**Lamm** lamb
**Leber** liver
**Nockerln** small dumplings
**Paradieser** tomatoes
**Rahm** cream
**Rindfleisch** beef
**Schinken** ham
**Schweine-fleisch** pork
**Topfen** cream cheese
**Zwiebeln** onions

# WHERE TO EAT

Restaurants are listed alphabetically. Price categories are based on the cost, per person, of a dinner comprising starter, mid-priced main course and dessert (not including wine, coffee, or service) and are indicated as follows:

€€€    **over 45 euros**
€€    **20–45 euros**
€    **20 euros and under**

## RESTAURANTS
### The Innere Stadt (District 1)

**Al Borgo €€** *1, An Der Hulben 1, tel: 01-512 855;* www.alborgo.at. Specialising in Mediterranean cuisine, Al Borgo's chef serves Italian specialties with a creative twist, using only top-quality fresh local ingredients. An ever-changing seasonal menu.

**Artner am Franziskanerplatz €€€** *1, Franziskanerplatz 5, tel: 01-503 5034;* www.artner.co.at. Sister restaurant to the more experimental Artner in the 4th district, this eatery plates up some wonderful Austrian fare, including regional specialities from Styria. Finish off with a Burgenland wine, served in an atmospheric brick-lined cellar with a chic interior design.

**Beim Czaak €€** *1, Postgasse 15, tel: 01-513 7215;* www.czaak.com. A friendly *Beisl* with helpful staff tucked away behind the Old University, hence popular with students. The hearty menu includes superb *Tafelspitz*, sinful desserts and an excellent selection of beers.

**Bristol Lounge €€€** *1, Kärntner Ring 1, tel: 01-5151 6553;* www.bristol-lounge. at. Conveniently located next to the Vienna Opera, Bristol Hotel's restaurant enjoys a lovely historic Art Déco ambiance. In cold weather a fire crackles in the large fireplace. Chef Manuel Gratzl serves excellent traditional Austrian dishes and imaginative interpretations of international classics.

**Cantinetta Antinori €€€** *1, Jasomirgottstrasse 3–5, tel: 01-5337 722;* www. cantinetta-antinori.com/vienna-2. Run by the famous Tuscan wine-producing family, this is a slick Italian restaurant serving reliable food. Closely packed tables are not for the shy. The Chianti wines produced by the owners are a must.

**Clementine €€€** *1, Coburgbastei 4, tel: 01-5181 8130;* www.palais-coburg.com. One of the most impressive places to eat in the city in a rather classy palace hotel. The dining room is set in a beautiful glass house, and dishes up great Austrian classics with a twist, and there is an amazing selection of wines.

**ef16 €€** *1, Fleischmarkt 16, tel: 01-513 2318;* www.ef16.at. The vaulted interior and garden courtyard at ef16 is the perfect setting for enjoying innovative Austrian cooking full of authenticity, which attaches importance to regional and seasonal local products.

**Esterhazy Keller €€** *1, Haarhof 1, tel: 01-533 3482;* www.esterhazykeller.at. A *Stadtheurigen* in a dark cellar; take the winding stairs down from the small doorway. Typical belt-stretching food and local wines. Atmospheric in a very Viennese sort of way.

**Gasthaus Pöschl €€** *1, Weihburggasse 17, tel: 01-513 5288.* Popular at lunchtime with local workers, it serves up tasty home-cooked traditional Austrian fare and has a good range of drinks.

**Griechenbeisl €€** *1, Fleischmarkt 11, tel: 01-533 1977;* www.griechenbeisl.at. This tavern was first recorded in 1447 and its small vaulted rooms have been a public house ever since. First frequented by Levantine and Greek merchants (hence the name), who inhabited Fleishmarkt, it was subsequently visited by many famous musicians and writers. Now the classic Viennese food is largely served up to tourists.

**Hansen €€** *1, Wipplingerstrasse 34, tel: 01-532 0542;* www.hansen.co.at. Set in the vaulted cellars underneath Theophil Hansen's Borse building, and sharing the space with the florist Lederleitner, this is a lovely place for a meal. The food is modern Mediterranean with a slight Austrian twist and it is a great place for breakfast (served until 11.30am).

**Loca €€€** *1, Stubenbastei 1, tel: 01-512 1172*. The six-course surprise tasting menu is really worth a try and is perfectly paired with wine.

**Palmenhaus €€** *1, Burggarten 1, tel: 01-533 1033;* www.palmenhaus.at. This spectacular *Jugendstil* glasshouse now houses a restaurant and café. Good modern European dishes and a few Viennese classics although things can get quite crowded and noisy the later it gets.

**Pfudl €€** *1, Bäckerstrasse 22, tel: 01-512 6705;* www.gasthauspfudl.com. This *Beisl* has a rural atmosphere and finely prepared traditional Viennese cuisine, topped off with speedy service and a meagre bill.

**Plachutta €€€** *1, Wollzeile 38, tel: 01-512 1577;* www.plachutta.at. A long-standing central restaurant that is particularly famous for its *Tafelspitz* although the other Viennese classics are not bad either.

**Reinthaler €€** *1, Dorotheergasse 2, tel: 01-513 1249;* www.reinthalersbeisl. com. Classic city-centre *Beisl*, very popular with the Viennese for the hearty portions and quality of the food.

**Salonplafond im MAK €€** *1, Stubenring 5, tel: 01-226 0046;* www.salonpla-fond.wien. The café and restaurant of the Museum of Applied Arts has been beautifully designed and turns out excellent modern takes on classic Austrian dishes as well as a good selection of wines.

**Trzesniewski €** *1, Dorotheergasse 1, tel: 01-512 3291;* www.trzesniewski.at. With a great preserved interior this place specialises in the beloved Viennese open-faced sandwich, with toppings such as egg, red onion, salmon or crab. Diners cluster around chest-high tables and eat standing up; beer is the drink of choice here.

**Wrenkh €€** *1, Bauernmarkt 10, tel: 01-533 1526;* www.wrenkh-wien.at. A place for vegetarians and healthy eaters with top-notch food, excellent wines and a cosy ambience.

**Zu den 3 Hacken €€** *1, Singerstrasse 28, tel: 01-512 5895;* www.zuden3hacken.at. A good place for lovers of traditional Viennese cooking. The menu is big, and so are the portions. Very popular with local diners, so advance booking may be necessary.

**Zum Schwarzen Kameel €€** *1, Bognergasse 5, tel: 01-533 8125;* www.kameel. at. This delicatessen and Art Nouveau restaurant is crammed with history – allegedly Beethoven used to eat here, though he probably wouldn't recognise today's gourmet menu which locals flock to savour.

## Around the Ringstrasse (Districts 2–9)

**Entler €€€** *4, Schlusselgasse 2, tel: 01-504 3585;* www.entler.at. Not far from the Taubstummengasse metro station, this highly recommended restaurant combines contemporary and traditional décor to set the perfect scene for some of the capital's best Austrian cuisine. Service is top-notch but be prepared to wait a little for your food as everything is prepared fresh.

**Gasthaus Wild €€** *3, Radetzkyplatz 1, tel: 01-920 9477.* This *Beisl* has been beautifully restored, keeping the original character. The food, which includes typical Viennese dishes, is excellent, as is the selection of beers and wines.

**Glacis Beisl €€** *7, Breitegasse 4, tel: 01-526 5660;* www.glacisbeisl.at. Part of the MuseumsQuartier complex, a busy modern space that serves up great Viennese food. Very popular so it's advisable to book.

**Kias Kitchen €€** *6, Gumpendorferstrasse 37, tel: 676 3850020;* www.kiaskitchen.org. Chef Kias delivers experimental Brazilian cuisine with influences from around the world. The menu changes weekly, and everything is homemade with organic and local ingredients.

**Ramen Makotoya €€** *6, Reichsratsstrasse, tel: 01-402 8903;* www.ramenmakotoya.at. This Japanese franchise brings mighty flavours to Vienna's city centre. As the name suggests, they specialise in ramen – chicken, beef, vegan, spicy, or whatever you're craving.

**Schnattl €€€** *8, Lange Gasse 40, tel: 01-405 3400;* www.schnattl.com. Top contemporary Austrian cuisine bursting with fresh and delicate flavours. The interior is a pleasant and airy traditional space and the selection of wines is superb.

**Schweizerhaus** € *2, Prater 116, tel: 01-728 01520;* www.schweizerhaus. at. Huge portions of belly-extending roast pork knuckle (known as *Stelze*) served up in a madly busy eating house; you can also relax with a draught beer in the tree-shaded garden.

**Silberwirt** €€ *5, Schlossgasse 21, tel: 01-544 4907;* www.silberwirt.at. This very popular *Beisl* is packed at weekends with all kinds of folk. Good, traditional fare served up in a charming courtyard setting, all at a decent price.

**Steirereck im Wien** €€€ *3, Am Heumarkt 2a, tel: 01-713 3168;* www.steirereck.at. One of Austria's top restaurants, now relocated to a beautifully designed modern building overlooking the Stadtpark. It specialises in creative twists on Austrian classics. Try the cheaper lunch menu, or sample the huge range of cheeses in the Meierei.

**Ubl** €€ *4, Pressgasse 26, tel: 01-587 6437.* Old-fashioned establishment serving good quality Schnitzels and other classic Austrian fare, including *Zwiebel-rostbraten* and *Tafelspitz*.

**Wiener Wiaz Haus** €€ *4, Karlsgasse 22, tel: 01-505 4507;* www.wiener-wiazhaus.com. Red checked tablecloths and posters on the wall reflect a cosy charm at this family-run, Austrian restaurant. The goulash and Apple Strudel are popular and be sure to try the homemade fruit vodka. The place gets busy, so booking is a must.

**Witwe Bolte** €€ *7, Gutenberggasse 13, tel: 01-523 1450;* www.witwebolte.at. Viennese home-style cooking at its best in one of the city's oldest and simplest *Beisln*. Located in the interesting Spittleberg district.

## Further Afield

**Buschenschank Kroiss** € *19, Sieveringer Strasse 108, tel: 01-320 3992.* If you have a particular interest in genuine local grape varieties, then don't miss this *Heuriger*. *Weissburgunder, roter Zweigelt* and *Grüner Veltliner* are among those on offer, while *Gemischter Satz* is a blend of different grape varieties that are picked and pressed together.

**Fuhrgassl-Huber €€** *19, Neustift am Walde 68, tel: 01-440 1405;* www.fuhrgassl-huber.at. If you fancy a rustic setting, don't miss the earthy atmosphere of this *Heuriger*. On days when it's too cold to sit outside in the magnificent garden, warm yourself indoors with a plate of suckling pig, grilled chicken or other choice items from the buffet.

**Gerhard Klager €€** *21, Stammersdorfer Strasse 14, tel: 01-292 4107;* www.weingutklager.at. This *Heuriger* is particularly good for children, who can play in the playground while the adults sample fine wines and buffet food. If you're driving, try the delicious low-alcohol version.

## VIENNESE CAFÉS

**Aida €** *1, Singerstrasse 1, tel: 01-890 8988-210;* www.aida.at. Aida is a chain themed in shocking pink with 1950s decor. The coffee is wonderful (some say the best) and the *patisserie* is a dream.

**Alt Wien €** *1, Bäckerstrasse 9, tel: 01-512 5222;* www.kaffeealtwien.at. A café bordering on a *Beisl* with a deliberately decadent and dingy atmosphere. It offers a mouth-watering selection of snacks. You may come across an interesting literary clientele in the evenings.

**Bräunerhof €** *1, Stallburggasse 2, tel: 01-512 3893.* Popular city-centre café with a wide selection of *Torten*.

**Café Central €** *1, Herrengasse 14 (Palais Ferstel), tel: 01-533 3763 24;* www.palaisevents.at. The haunt of artists and intellectuals from times past, including Leon Trotsky and Peter Altenberg. Now a bit of a tourist trap and pricey.

**Café Drechsler €** *6, Linke Wienzeile 22, tel: 01-512 3893;* www.cafedrechsler.at. This former coffee house legend has been providing hot comfort to the market traders across the road for years. The food is good and so are the prices.

**Demel k.u.k Hofzuckerbäcker €** *1, Kohlmarkt 14, tel: 01-535 1717;* www.demel.at. Candies, crowds and cakes since 1796. Demel was, by appointment, pastry chef to Franz Joseph. It serves some of the best cakes in town.

**Diglas €** *1, Wollzeile 10, tel: 01-512 5765;* www.diglas.at. A venerable coffee house with very comfortable seats and huge slabs of cake. One of the city's best and conveniently located near Stephansplatz.

**Frauenhuber €** *1, Himmelpfortgasse 6, tel: 01-512 5353;* www.cafefrauenhuber.at. One of Vienna's oldest cafés (1824) and one of the prettiest. It's said that Mozart performed here and Beethoven was a regular.

**Hawelka €** *1, Dorotheergasse 6, tel: 01-512 8230;* www.hawelka.at. A dark and atmospheric café with a central location but today without its former artist patrons.

**Kleines Café €** *1, Franziskanerplatz 3.* As the name suggests this is a tiny place, but beautifully designed and popular with local intellectuals. There is overspill outside in the square during summer.

**Landtmann €** *1, Universitätsring 4, tel: 01-2410 0120;* www.landtmann.at. Always the most prestigious of the Ringstrasse cafés, next door to the Burgtheater.

**Meinl Café €** *1, Graben 19, tel: 01-532 3334;* www.meinlamgraben.at. Taking advantage of its place at Vienna's most prestigious food store, the eponymous Meinl serves up 30 varieties of freshy ground coffee, sweet treats and light snacks.

**Mozart €** *1, Albertinaplatz 2, tel: 01-2410 0200;* www.cafe-mozart.at. There's been a café here since 1794. In Biedermeier times it was a meeting place for artists.

**Museum €** *1, Operngasse 7, tel: 01-2410 0620;* www.cafemuseum.at. Popular with arts students and lecturers, with a disastrously over-renovated Adolf Loos interior.

**Prückel €** *1, Stubenring 24, tel: 01-512 6115.* Situated opposite the Museum of Fine Arts, this is a fine old Viennese café, with a 1950s interior, serving a full menu.

**Sperl €** *6, Gumpendorfer Strasse 11, tel: 01-586 4158;* www.cafesperl.at. Popular with Franz Lehár, and the meeting place of the stars, Sperl still attracts theatre people and literary types. Billiards and card tables.

# TRAVEL ESSENTIALS

## PRACTICAL INFORMATION

# A

## ACCESSIBLE TRAVEL

Vienna has implemented a great many schemes to enable wheelchair access. Most hotels have wheelchair access and some have rooms adapted for those with accessibility requirements, though it would be wise to question the manager before making a reservation to ensure that the room is suitable. Older buses and trams are not accessible, though many U-Bahn stations are. The Vienna Tourist Board (www.wien.info) can provide up-to-date information and has a list of sights and attractions with wheelchair access – the Riesenrad (Ferris wheel) is accessible. Local voluntary organisations may also offer help.

Mobility4ever (www.mobile4ever.at) offer mobility electric scooters to rent – delivery directly to the hotel or excursion location.

## ACCOMMODATION

The Vienna Tourist Board (www.wien.info) publishes a list of hotels, *Pensionen* (guest houses) and *Saison Hotels* (student hostels used as hotels from July to September) with details about amenities, prices and classifications. You can pick it up, along with a free city map, from the Austrian Tourist Board in your country or from travel agents. Tourist information offices in Vienna (see page 129) can book rooms for you, for a small fee. Be aware that if you cancel your reservation, all hotels have the right to charge a cancellation fee.

The more homely atmosphere of a pension in Vienna makes it popular for longer stays, though, as with some of the cheaper hotels, not all of them have rooms with private baths. Apartments are also available for longer stays. It is always advisable to book ahead, especially for travel from Easter to the end of September, and at Christmas and New Year. It is also possible to stay in private homes on a bed-and-breakfast basis. This is an especially attractive option in some of the smaller villages around Vienna. The famous old luxury hotels around the Opera are often fully booked by a long-established clientele, so reservations are necessary well in advance.

a guest house **eine Pension**
a single/double room **ein Einzel-/Doppelzimmer**
with/without bath (shower) **mit/ohne Bad (Dusche)**
What's the rate per night? **Was kostet eine Übernachtung?**

# AIRPORT

Vienna's airport, **Wien-Schwechat Airport** (VIE, www.viennaairport.com) is located about 20km (12 miles) from the centre of Vienna and handles domestic as well as international flights.

The City Airport Train (CAT, www.cityairporttrain.com), which leaves every 30 minutes, provides a high-speed (16 minutes) connection to the City Air Terminal at Landstrasse (Wien Mitte). There is also the Schnellbahn (S-Bahn), which takes longer but is much cheaper. Airport shuttle buses leave approximately every 30 minutes for major transport hubs in the city centre. The Airport Service Wien is a private shuttle service that takes you to your exact address (tel: 676 786 1065, www.vienna-airport-cab.at). A taxi to the city centre should cost around €36-40.

Where can I find a taxi? **Wo finde ich ein Taxi?**
How much is it to the centre? **Wieviel kostet es ins Zentrum?**
Does this bus go to the railway station? **Fährt dieser Bus zum Bahnhof?**

# B

# BICYCLE RENTAL

Bicycles are available to rent from bike hire shops and at mainline railway stations. Pedal Power (Bösendorferstrasse 5, www.pedalpower.at) hires out bikes and organises guided tours (advance booking required) as does **Vienna Ex-**

**plorer** (Franz-Josefs-Kai 45, www.viennaexplorer.com). Expect to pay around €30 a day, about 10 percent less if you are a student.

# BUDGETING FOR YOUR TRIP

When budgeting for a trip to Vienna, count on most things being a touch more expensive than in the UK. However, this depends on the exchange rate between the pound and the euro.

A great way to save money is to buy a **Vienna Card** which provides reduced admission and other benefits at over 200 museums and sights, hotels, theatres, concert halls, shops, restaurants, cafés and wine gardens *(Heuriger)*; unlimited travel by underground, bus and tram, and a reduction on the shuttle bus to/from the city centre.

The card valid for 24 hours costs €17 while the 48-hour costs €25 and 72-hour card €29. It can be purchased at Vienna Airport and at hotels and tourist information offices (www.wien.info).

To give you an idea of what you can expect to pay for what, here is a short list of average prices. They can only be approximate, however, as in Austria, too, inflation creeps relentlessly up.

**Hotels.** See Recommended Hotels, page 132. For a night in a double room in a hotel with a bath or a shower including breakfast, you can expect prices to start at around €150, though you may find cheaper accommodation if you are prepared to look at hostels or at hotels further outside of the centre. There is no real maximum price on hotel rooms and there are many luxurious options; however, in our Where To Stay chapter we have listed a range that reaches up to around the €350 mark.

**Meals.** The average cost of a standard meal, including a glass of wine is between €25 and €35 per person.

**Museums.** Entrance fees vary considerably. Concessions are available at many museums for holders of the Vienna Card. Entrance for children under six is generally free. There is a reduction for schoolchildren (passport required) and students (international student identity card required).

**Public transport.** €2.40 for single ticket, €8 for a 24-hour ticket, €17.10 for a 72-hour ticket. Children under six years old travel free.

# C

## CAMPING

For information about campsites, camping and caravanning, www.campsite.
at is a helpful websites and makes for a very good place to start. Of camping
sites located around the city, there is one that is open all year (other than
February): Wien West, Hüttelbergstrasse 40 and 80, tel: 914 2314. Another
good camping site is: Camping Neue Donau, Am Kleehäufel, tel: 202 4010
(mid-Apr–Oct). The website www.campingwien.at contains useful information about both sites.

## CAR RENTAL/HIRE (see also Driving)

For travelling inside the city, parking would make a car more of a hindrance
than an asset, but having a car is certainly useful for excursions out to the
Wienerwald and the Danube Valley.

Though some local firms may offer lower prices than Avis, Budget,
Europcar and Hertz, these international agencies are more likely to let
you return the car elsewhere in the country at no extra cost. The best
deals can usually be found online or through the airline you are using
to reach Vienna. The average daily hire charge for a medium-sized car is
between €40–€60.

Third-party insurance is compulsory, but full cover is recommended. To
avoid unpleasant surprises, make sure the price quoted includes all the necessary insurance and taxes. To hire a car, you must show your driving licence
(held for at least a year) and passport. You also need a major credit card, or a
large deposit will be required. The minimum age for renting cars ranges from
20 to 23.

**Avis** www.avis.at

**Budget** www.budget.at

**Megadrive** www.megadrive.at

**Sixt** www.sixt.at

**Hertz** www.hertz.at

> I'd like to rent a car **Ich möchte bitte ein Auto mieten**
> today **für heute**
> tomorrow **für morgen**
> for a week **für eine Woche**

## CLIMATE

Spring is Vienna's most pleasant season. Chestnut trees and white lilacs are in blossom for the city's music festival. In July and August the Viennese leave the city relatively free for visitors, and in autumn, the Wienerwald is in splendid colour for the *Heuriger* wine gardens, and the opera and theatre season in the city centre. Even in winter Vienna is worth the trip for a marvellous white Christmas, despite the cold east wind.

The chart shows Vienna's average monthly temperatures:

|      | J  | F  | M  | A  | M  | J  | J  | A  | S  | O  | N  | D  |
|------|----|----|----|----|----|----|----|----|----|----|----|----|
| °F   | 30 | 34 | 41 | 50 | 59 | 64 | 68 | 66 | 61 | 50 | 41 | 34 |
| °C   | -1 | 1  | 5  | 10 | 15 | 18 | 20 | 19 | 16 | 10 | 5  | 1  |

## CLOTHING

To best prepare for the extremes of Vienna's weather, take light cottons for the very hot summer afternoons and your warmest woollen layers for the bitter winter. The wind off the steppe can whip through at any time; so even in the middle of the summer, for an occasional cool evening, take a sweater and rain-coat. The Viennese like to dress up for the theatre, concerts and opera, but a dark suit or cocktail dress is nearly always appropriate. A dinner jacket or evening dress may be worn on very special occasions, such as for premieres and galas.

## CRIME AND SAFETY

Austria is a rather convention-bound society and the level of crime, though rising, is less than in some comparable countries. Nevertheless, all the usual precautions should be taken whilst travelling in a foreign country: valuables should ideally be left in a safe provided at the hotel and the interiors of parked cars should be cleared of tempting objects. You should carry some sort of ID on your person at all times, and it is a good idea to make a photocopy of your passport and have a record of the numbers of your credit, and any other, cards in case of loss or theft. Report thefts and incidents to the police *(Polizei)* who are generally very helpful to visitors from Western countries.

I want to report a theft. **Ich möchte einen Diebstahl melden.**

# D

## DRIVING (See also Car Rental/Hire)

To bring your car into Austria you will need:
- valid driving licence (national licence for Europeans);
- car registration papers;
- national identity sticker for your car;
- red warning triangle in case of breakdown;
- first-aid kit;
- reflective jacket.

Road conditions are by and large very good in Austria, only remote country roads are not paved.

**Driving regulations.** Drive on the right, pass on the left. Although drivers in Austria follow the same basic rules which apply in other countries that drive on the right, there are some rules that might differ somewhat:
- On the motorway *(Autobahn)* passing another vehicle on its right is prohibited.
- Vehicles coming from the right have priority at crossroads without other signals.
- Trams have priority, even when coming from the left.
- You must wear seatbelts.

• Children under the age of 12 may not sit in the front, and must use a special safety seat.
• It is prohibited to use your horn (day or night) in town.
• Vehicles must halt behind trams when they are slowing down to stop and when loading or unloading passengers.
• Drink-driving is a very serious offence in Austria. The permissible alcohol level in the blood is 0.5 percent.

---

driving licence **Führerschein**
car registration papers **Zulassungsschein**
green card **Grüne Karte**
Where's the nearest car park, please? **Wo ist der nächste Parkplatz, bitte?**
Can I park here? **Darf ich hier parken?**
Are we on the right road for...? **Sind wir auf der richtigen Strasse nach...?**
Check the oil/tyres/battery, please. **Öl/Reifen/Batterie prüfen, bitte.**
I've had a breakdown. **Ich habe eine Panne.**
There's been an accident. **Es ist ein Unfall passiert.**

---

**Speed limits.** On motorways (expressways) 130kmh (81mph) or 100kmh (62mph); on other roads 100kmh or 80kmh (50mph); in built-up areas 50kmh (31mph); with caravan (trailer) 80kmh (50mph) on the open road; with studded tyres 100kmh (62mph) on motorways, 80kmh (50mph) on other roads.

**Parking.** If at all possible, use public transport within the Gürtel (outer ring road) since one-way streets and traffic jams add confusion within the city, where there is a lack of parking space. A single short-stay parking zone requiring the purchase of a parking ticket came into force across almost the entire Vienna metropolitan area in March: Monday to Friday 9am to 10pm, maximum duration two hours. Tickets are available at transport ticket offices, tourist information centre  and tobacco shops (Tabaktrafik).

**Breakdowns.** The warning triangle must be displayed to indicate a broken-down vehicle and hazard lights must be switched on. Assistance can be obtained by calling the ÖAMTC (Austrian Automobile Club), tel: 120, or ARBÖ (Austrian Drivers' Association), tel: 123. Accidents involving injury must be reported to the police.

**Anfang** (Parking) Start
**Ausfahrt** Exit
**Aussicht** Viewpoint
**Bau-arbeiten** Road works
**Einbahn-strasse** One way
**Ende** (Parking) End
**Fahrbahn-wechsel** Change lanes
**Fussgänger** Pedestrians
**Gefahr** Danger
**Geradeaus** Straight on
**Glatteis** Slippery roads
**Halten-verboten** No stopping
**Licht einschalten** Use headlights
**Ortsende** Town ends
**Parken erlaubt** Parking allowed
**Rechts, links einbiegen** Turn right, left
**Rollsplitt** Loose gravel
**Sackgasse** No through road
**Spital** Hospital
**Steinschlag** Falling stones
**Umleitung** Diversion
**Vorfahrt** Priority
**Vorsicht** Caution
**Werktags von 7 bis 17 Uhr** Weekdays 7am to 5pm
**Zufahrt gestattet** Entrance permitted

# E

## ELECTRICITY

You'll need an adapter for most British and US plugs: Austrian sockets have round holes. Electricity supplies are 220 volt, and US equipment will require a transformer. Shaver outlets are generally dual voltage.

## EMBASSIES AND CONSULATES

Contact your consulate or embassy only for real emergencies, such as loss of a passport or all your money, a serious accident or trouble with the police.

**Australia:** Gertrude-Fröhlich-Sandnerstrasse 2, 1100 Vienna, tel: 01-506 740, www.austria.embassy.gov.au

**Canada:** Laurenzerberg 2, 1010 Vienna; tel: 01-531 383 000; www.canadainternational.gc.ca

**Ireland:** Rotenturmstrasse 16–18, 1010 Vienna; tel: 01-715 4246; www.embassyofireland.at

**New Zealand:** The ICON, Tower 24, Wiedner Gürtel 13, 1100 Vienna; tel: 01-505 3021; www.nzembassy.com/austria

**South Africa:** Sandgasse 33, 1190 Vienna; tel: 01-320 6493; www.suedafrikabotschaft.at

**UK:** Jauresgasse 12, 1030 Vienna; tel: 01-716 130; www.gov.uk/world/austria

**US:** Boltzmanngasse 16, 1090 Vienna; tel: 01-313 390; www.usembassy.gov

## EMERGENCIES (See also Crime and Safety and Police)

In an emergency the pan-European emergency number **112** should be called.

The following are the old numbers for the various emergency services that also still work.

Police **133**

Fire **122**

Ambulance **144**

I need a doctor/dentist. **Ich brauche einen Arzt/ Zahnarzt.**
ambulance **Krankenwagen**
Fire! **Feuer!**
Help! **Hilfe!**
hospital **Spital**
police **Polizei**

# G

## GETTING THERE

**By Air:** There is regular service to Vienna from various centres in the UK. Austrian Airlines (www.austrian.com) and British Airways (www.ba.com) operate scheduled direct flights from London Heathrow. Flying time from London is two and a half hours. The low-cost airline Ryanair (www.ryanair.com) flies from London Stansted, Bristol, Manchester and Edinburgh to Vienna, while easyJet (www.easyjet.com) operate a service to Salzburg from London Gatwick. The train journey from Salzburg to Vienna takes three hours. Ryanair also fly to Bratislava in Slovakia, a short hop across the border from Vienna.

In addition to non-stop flights from New York and Chicago, there is a scheduled service from more than 40 American cities as well as a dozen cities in Canada to European gateway destinations from which you can make connections to Vienna.

**By Car:** The quickest route to Vienna from the UK is via Calais through Brussels, Cologne, Nuremburg, Passau and Linz (1300km (800 miles), although there are more attractive routes, such as Die Romantische Strasse (the Romantic Road), via Rothenburg ob der Tauber, through the countryside. There are regular daily car ferry departures from Dover to Calais, or you can put your car on the train and travel through the Channel Tunnel from Folkestone to Calais in 35 minutes.

Depending from which direction you come, you might be able to put your car on the train for part of the journey. In the summer a car-train (Autozug; www.autozug-sylt.de) service links Vienna with cities in Germany and Italy.

Arriving with the car-train allows you to avoid traffic jams around Vienna and brings you close to the town centre.

The Austrian Federal Railways (www.oebb.at) operates car-trains between Vienna and Feldkirch (overnight service with couchettes also available), Linz, Villach and Innsbruck and Salzburg (both during the ski season only).

**By Coach:** For details of coach services to Vienna from London and other European cities contact Eurolines (www.eurolines.de).

**By Train:** The Köln–Vienna sleeper (book online at www.bahn.de) is the easiest way to reach Austria from London (connect via Brussels on Eurostar) and it takes about 13 hours; the entire trip, London to Vienna, takes about 20 hours. The cabins are very comfortable and couchettes are also available.

The Eurail Austria Pass allows unlimited travel on Austrian Railways; available for 3-8 days travel within one month. Contact Austrian Federal Railways for details (www.eurail.com).

## GUIDES AND TOURS

The most romantic tour of Vienna is in the famous horse-drawn *Fiaker* cab. These are usually parked at the Michaelerplatz, Stephansplatz, Petersplatz, or near the Albertina and will take you around the major sightseeing spots. Make sure you agree on the cost of the trip before you begin.

**Vienna Sightseeing** bus tours, with English commentary, are conveniently run on a hop-on/hop-off basis on three sightseeing routes with up to 30 stops. Buy tickets (from €27) online at www.viennasightseeing.at.

The Tourist Information Board organises guided **theme tours on foot** (*Wiener Spaziergänge*, www.wienguide.at), often with English-speaking guides. Each tour lasts approximately 90 minutes. They cover all manner of special interests: Medieval Vienna, Hundertwasser and modern architecture, Jewish Vienna, *Jugendstil*, the *Musikmeile* (Music Mile) a classical music walk, and *Der Dritte Mann* (The Third Man), which follows in the footsteps of the classic 1949 film. Most hotels can arrange – at a price – for English-speaking guides or interpreters to accompany you on your way around the city. Otherwise contact the Vienna Tourist Board for more information or **Vienna Guide Service**, www.guides-in-vienna.at.

We'd like an English-speaking guide. **Wir möchten einen englisch-sprachigen Fremdenführer.**
I need an English interpreter. **Ich brauche einen Dolmetscher für Englisch.**
How long will the ride take? **Wie lange dauert die Fahrt?**
What does it cost? **Was kostet es?**

# H

## HEALTH AND MEDICAL CARE

No special precautions need to be taken when travelling to Austria, which is generally a very safe, clean and healthy country with excellent medical services, but check the latest Covid vaccination requirements before travelling. Emergency medical care is free of charge for EU citizens, though you may have to pay for medicines. Before travelling, British subjects should obtain a free Global Health Insurance Card (apply online at www.gov.uk/global-health-insurance-card). Citizens of countries outside the EU should ensure that they are covered by a comprehensive private health insurance policy. Such insurance is worth considering in any case in order to cover any longer-term problems and to ensure prompt repatriation if necessary. Minor health problems can often be dealt with by visiting a pharmacy *(Apotheke)*. These sport a green cross and/or snake and staff sign. In big cities several stay open all night and the addresses should be posted in the windows of those that close. In case of accident or serious illness, call the ambulance service on **144** or general emergency number **112**.

Where is there a pharmacy on duty? **Wo ist die diensthabende Apotheke?**

# L

## LANGUAGE

Austria is German-speaking, but English is also very widely understood and spoken. The *Berlitz German Phrase Book and Dictionary* covers most situations you're likely to encounter in Austria.

## LGBTQ+ TRAVELLERS

This sophisticated capital has a relatively friendly attitude towards the LGBTQ+ community. Since 1996, the Regenbogen (Rainbow) Parade has been held every June on the Ringstrasse.

A list of restaurants, hotels and bars which welcome LGBTQ+ identifying travellers is provided at many websites, including www.travelgay.com/destination/gay-austria, www.travelgayeurope.com/gay-map-of-vienna and www.patroc.com/vienna.

Two places for information are: Heumühlgasse 14/1, 1040 Vienna, tel: 01-216 6604, www.hosiwien.at, and Rosa Lila Villa, 6, Linke Wienzeile 102, tel: 01-586 8150, www.dievilla.at. A 'Gay and Lesbian Guide for Vienna' is available for download from the city's tourism website, www.wien.info.

# M

## MAPS

The Tourist Information Board gives away excellent street-maps of the city. Most useful will always be a large-scale map of the Innere Stadt (Inner City) and of the U-Bahn network.

## MEDIA

Major hotels and most kiosks in the First District sell English-language daily newspapers from London, the *Wall Street Journal* and *USA Today*, and the news magazines.

TV in the major hotels usually has CNN and BBC World news services, along with other major European channels. The state-run broadcaster for TV and radio is ÖRF (www.orf.at).

# MONEY

The euro (€) is the official currency used in Austria. Notes are denominated in 5, 10, 20, 50, 100 and 500 euros (last two rarely seen); coins in 1 and 2 euros and 1, 2, 5, 10, 20 and 50 cents.

**Changing money.** The easiest way to obtain euros is with a suitable debit/credit card at a cash machine *(Geldautomat)*, but note that not all cards are accepted at all machines and that most banks charge for this service. Foreign currency can be changed at practically any bank or savings bank *(Sparkasse)*. As well as bureaux de change, travel agencies and hotels will often change money, though the rate is not likely to be a favourable one. Travellers' cheques are widely accepted but probably not worth the hassle for the protection they provide.

**Credit cards.** Cash is still popular in Austria, but in the wake of the Covid pandemic major credit and debit cards are much more widely accepted – although still not universally. American Express and the likes may not be accepted everywhere. Occasionally you may come across an establishment that only takes one type of card. Tipping in cash is appreciated.

> I want to change some pounds/dollars **Ich möchte Pfund/ Dollar wechseln.**
> Do you accept travellers' cheques? **Nehmen Sie Reiseschecks an?**
> Where's the nearest ATM, please? **Wo ist der nächste Geldautomat, bitte?**

# OPENING HOURS

**Banks.** Monday to Friday 8am–3pm, possibly with later opening on Thursday.

**Museums.** Most museums open at 9am or 10am and close at 5pm or 6pm, though there may be late opening on one day a week. Many are closed all day Monday. See individual listings in the Where to Go section.

**Post offices.** Monday to Friday 8am–6pm.

**Shops.** Official shop opening hours are Monday to Friday 9am–6pm with early closing on Saturday. Small shops close at lunchtime while larger establishments may open earlier and stay open longer one evening a week. In areas frequented by large groups of tourists, however, shops may remain open as long as there is a chance of custom. Shops located at airports and main railway stations keep longer hours.

# P

## POLICE (see also Crime and Safety and Emergencies)

Vienna's police wear dark blue or black uniforms, and drive silver cars. Traffic police wear white caps. Street parking is supervised by Politessen (traffic wardens) in blue jackets and white hats. If you are fined for any reason, the police have the right to ask you to pay on the spot. In emergencies, call **133** or **112**. Vienna's main police station is at Schottenring 7-9.

Where is the nearest police station, please? **Wo ist die nächste Polizei-wache, bitte?**

## POST OFFICE

Apart from regular post office hours (Monday–Friday 8am–6pm), larger post offices and those at main railway stations (Hauptbahnhof, Westbahnhof and Franz Josefs-Bahnhof) may stay open late on Saturday. The postal centre at Vienna airport offers an automated 24-hour service for registered, air and express mail (payment by debit/credit card). The Central Post Office is at Fleischmarkt 19. Letterboxes and post office signs are coloured yellow.

express (special delivery) **Express/Eilbote**
A stamp for this letter/postcard, please. **Eine Marke für diesen Brief/diese Postkarte, bitte.**

## PUBLIC HOLIDAYS

**1 January** *Neujahr* New Year's Day

**6 January** *Dreikönigstag* Epiphany

**March/April** *Ostermontag* Easter Monday

**1 May** *Tag der Arbeit* May Day/Labour Day

**May/June** *Christi Himmelfahrt* Ascension Day

**May/June** *Pfingstmontag* Whit Monday

**June** *Fronleichnam* Corpus Christi

**15 August** *Mariä Himmelfahrt* Assumption Day

**26 October** *Nationalfeiertag* National Day

**1 November** *Allerheiligen* All Saints Day

**8 December** *Maria Empfägnis* Immaculate Conception

**25 December** *Weihnachtsfeiertag* Christmas Day

**26 December** *Weihnachtsfeiertag (2)* St Stephen's Day

# T

## TELEPHONES

To call Vienna from abroad, dial 0043 followed by the area code (1) and the number.

To make an international call from Austria, dial 00 followed by the country code, area code and number.

Within Austria, to make a call from Vienna to another dial the relevant area code starting with zero, then the subscriber number. You do not need the area code when dialling within the same city/code area.

Getting a local mobile phone SIM card is probably the best way to stay connected in Vienna. Such cards can be bought from major electronics stores, all phone companies, and quite a few chain stores. As Austria is a member of the EU, and even post-Brexit, roaming charges remain relatively low.

## TIME ZONE

Austria follows Central European Time (GMT +1 hour) and in summer an hour is added for daylight saving.

See the box to compare the time in Vienna with other cities in the world.

| New York | London | **Vienna** | Jo'burg | Sydney | Auckland |
|----------|--------|-----------|---------|--------|----------|
| 6am | 11am | **noon** | noon | 8pm | 10pm |

## TIPPING

Although a service charge is included in restaurant bills, it is customary to round the amount up to the nearest euro or round figure. A small sum is also expected by cloakroom attendants, porters, chambermaids and tour guides.

## TOILETS

Well-maintained public toilets can usually be found in tourist hotspots and at railway stations. Keep small change handy in case there is a charge. Men's toilets are marked with the word 'Herren', Ladies with 'Damen'.

## TOURIST INFORMATION

The Austrian National Tourist Office (ANTO) dispenses comprehensive information both on the internet and in brochure form about where to go, what to see and where to stay and eat out in Vienna (and other Austrian cities). Visit the website at www.austria.info for more details. Offices are closed to the public but brochures can be ordered or downloaded from the regional offices listed on the ANTO website.

**Vienna Tourist Board.** The Tourist Information Office is conveniently located right behind the Vienna State Opera at Albertinaplatz 1/corner of Maysedergasse, tel: 24 555, www.wien.info, open 9am–6pm daily. Here they offer information and advice concerning your trip, free city maps and brochures, last minute accommodation reservations, sales of the Vienna City Card and tickets for events, and use of free Wifi. There is also a tourist information office at Vienna Airport (open 9am–6pm daily). For additional convenience, download the Vienna Tourist Board free app (ivie), a digital city guide.

## TRANSPORT

Maps for Vienna's excellent public transport system (buses, trams and underground rail) are available at main stops as well as at the central public transport information offices such as the one in Karlsplatz (Mon–Fri 6.30am–7pm).

**Tickets** (*Karten*) can be bought from a conductor or a machine onboard trams and buses (at an increased rate), from tobacconist's (*Tabaktrafik*), the booking office or a machine for mainline or city trains. A single ticket for a journey by tram, bus and underground, which covers changes made without interruption, costs €2.40. Tickets can be bought in advance online or from transport offices (*Verkehrsbetriebe*). Travel passes are available for 24 hours (€8), 48 hours (€14.10) and 72 hours (€17.10). For detailed tariff information, timetables, routes etc., see www.wienerlinien.at.

> Where is the nearest bus/tram stop, please? **Wo ist die nächste Bus-/Strassenbahn-Haltestelle, bitte?**
> I want a ticket to … **Ich will eine Fahrkarte nach …**
> single/return **einfache Fahrt/Rückfahrkarte**

# V

## VISAS AND ENTRY REQUIREMENTS

A valid passport is required for entry. Visitors from European Union (EU) countries, including the US, Canada, Australia and New Zealand do not require a visa, but nationals of other countries that do not have a reciprocal agreement with Austria do. For more information check www.bmeia.gv.at/london.

# W

## WEBSITES AND INTERNET ACCESS

Free Wi-fi is available at many bars, restaurants, cafés, shopping malls and most hotels. There are around 400 free WiFi hotspots across the city – the interactive City of Vienna map (www.wien.gv.at/stadtplan) shows all these hotspots. If you are taking your laptop along, consider purchasing a cheap local 'dongle' to access the internet anywhere there is a mobile phone signal. These can cost as little as €40 and even the lowest download speeds are fast enough for general browsing.

**Useful websites:**

**www.wien.info** One-stop shop for Vienna visitor information.

**www.austria.info** The Austrian Tourist Board site.

**www.wien.gv.at** The City of Vienna's website, lists information on all aspects of life in the city and is available in English.

**www.wienmuseum.at** For city museums.

**www.inyourpocket.com/austria/vienna** Expat restaurant, bar, hotel and entertainment reviews.

**www.viennatouristinformation.com** Comprehensive up to date information and listings.

# Y

## YOUTH HOSTELS

For details of organised youth hostels in Vienna, contact: Österreichischer Jugendherbergsverband (Austrian Youth Hostels Association), Zelinkagasse 12, 1010 Vienna, tel: 01-5333 5353, www.oejhv.at. Vienna also has a few independent backpacker hostels which can be booked through sites such as www.hostelworld.com.

**Vienna Youth Hostels:**

**Jugendherberge Wien Myrthengasse** – Myrthengasse 7, tel: 01-523 63160; hostel@chello.at; Dorm beds from €27.

**Jugendgästehaus Brigittenau** – Adalbert Stifter Strasse 73, tel: 01-332 8294; jgh.1200wien@chello.at; Dorm beds from €24.

**Wombats City Hostel –** Rechte Wienzeile 35, tel: 01-897 2336; www.wombats-hostels.com; Dorm beds from €20.

**Hostel Ruthensteiner** – Robert Hamerling Gasse 24, tel: 01-893 4202; www.hostelruthensteiner.com; Dorm beds from €19.

# WHERE TO STAY

Vienna's hotels easily compare in quality to those of other major European capitals. However, a slight shortage of accommodation, particularly during peak season – Christmas and New Year, and from Easter to the end of September – does mean that advance booking is advisable. Reservations can be made online and by telephone (country code 43 followed by area code 1), and are binding even if not confirmed in writing. Vienna's hotels used to be heavy on the frump, frill and the Biedermeier look, and while this is still prominent, a number of smart design hotels have opened up, lending a more contemporary vibe to the city's accommodation scene.

The hotels listed here are placed in four categories based on the approximate price in euros per night for a double room with private bath or shower unless otherwise stated. A service charge and taxes are included in the price. Breakfast is generally included in the rate, though it's best to check when you reserve as it is not always the case in pricier establishments, and this is usually a buffet of various cold meats and cheeses, cereals, bread, rolls, jam and coffee. Always confirm prices when booking. All the hotels listed take major credit cards; wheelchair access is widespread but not ubiquitous.

The district number precedes the street address.

| | |
|---|---|
| €€€€ | over 350 euros |
| €€€ | 250–350 euros |
| €€ | 150–250 euros |
| € | under 150 euros |

## THE INNERE STADT (DISTRICT 1)

**Astoria €€€** *1, Kärntnerstrasse 32–34, tel: 01-515 77; www.austria-trend.at.* A civilised and venerable old hotel immediately behind the Staatsoper. The 128 bedrooms are generously cut and comfortable with traditional décor. Some of them are accessible to guests with accessibility requirements. The hotel reopens at the end of 2023 following major refurbishment.

**Hotel Austria €€**  *1, Am Fleischmarkt 20, tel: 01-515 23;* www.hotelaustria-wien.at. Well maintained rooms in a very centrally placed hotel; those without bath are cheaper but all have free Wi-fi. A smart, friendly and tranquil retreat right in the city centre.

**Bristol €€€€**  *1, Kärntner Ring 1, tel: 01-515 160;* www.bristolvienna.com. An Art Nouveau building dating from 1884 providing a bit more cosiness than many other five-star hotels. Its restaurant, the Bristol Lounge, is known for its light Viennese cuisine and distinguished wine list. There are non-smoking rooms and wheelchair facilities for guests.

**Do & Co €€€€**  *1, Stephansplatz 12, tel: 01-24 188;* www.doco.com. This über-chic design hotel may just occupy the best spot of any Vienna hotel, on the upper storeys of the Haas Haus opposite the Stephansdom. Impeccable service and amazing views from the Bang & Olufsen-equipped cool, minimalist rooms are complimented by one of the most popular bars (the Onyx) and restaurants in the city. Although the rack rates are pretty high, you may get a good deal in low season.

**Hollman Beletage €€€**  *1, Köllnerhofgasse 6, tel: 01-961 1960;* www.hollmann-beletage.at. It is hard to recommend this small (26 rooms) hotel enough. It's super-central, and the rooms are contemporary and chic in their design and commendably well kept. The vibe is laid back and the reception even shuts down at night, leaving the guests to help themselves at the bar. Excellent value, and a hearty breakfast included in the price.

**Imperial €€€€**  *1, Kärntner Ring 16, tel: 01-501 100;* www.imperialvienna.com. Official guests of state, actors and leading pop stars bed down at the Imperial, with its 138 stylish rooms and suites. Definitely the place to be seen, and the restaurant is one of the best and most expensive in town (the café isn't bad either). All rooms can accommodate guests in wheelchairs.

**König von Ungarn €€€**  *1, Schulerstrasse 10, tel: 01-515 840;* www.kvu.at. Centrally located only metres from the Stephansdom, and over 400 years old, this hotel is packed with old-fashioned charm. It has everything you would expect of a four-star hotel, and the glass-roofed inner courtyard is particularly attractive. All rooms are wheelchair-friendly and there's free Wi-Fi throughout.

**Leo Grand €€€** *1, Bauernmarkt 1, tel: 01-90 606;* www.theleogrand.com. This unique hotel celebrates individualism and contemporary luxury in the interior design while retaining the history of the building. DOTS in the baroque courtyard is a beautiful space for drinks or fusion cuisine.

**Meridien €€€€** *1, Opernring 13, tel: 01-588 900;* www.marriott.com/en-us/hotels/viemd-le-meridien-vienna. Five-star luxury in a row of converted Ringstrasse buildings. The interiors have been beautifully designed, with clean modern lines. The restaurants come highly recommended as well.

**Nossek €€** *1, Graben 17, tel: 01-533 7041;* www.pension-nossek.at. Small, cosy Art Deco style pension in the heart of Vienna's shopping district. Its location in the pedestrian area makes this attractive building very popular so reservations are highly recommended in the high season.

**Palais Coburg €€€€** *1, Coburgbastei 4, tel: 01-518 18;* www.palais-coburg. com. Wallet-stretchingly expensive but wonderfully opulent, this mid-19th-century palace has been converted into a series of luxury suites. Everything is, as you would expect, very suave, with a fine-dining restaurant, pool and city centre garden.

**Park Hyatt Vienna €€€€** *1, Am Hof 2, tel: 01-227 401 234;* www.parkhyattvienna.com. A luxurious hotel in a 100-year-old listed building with marble floors, alabaster and shiny brass. 143 opulent rooms, including 41 suites and three accessible rooms. Facilities include a spa, sauna, fitness centre and an indoor pool. Excellent restaurant, the Bank.

**Pertschy €€€** *1, Habsburgergasse 5, tel: 01-534 490;* www.pertschy.com. A friendly small hotel right in the middle of the Innere Stadt. The rooms are very comfy and pleasant in a kitschy Viennese sort of way (which is all part of the charm) and breakfast is included in the price.

**Radisson Blu Style Hotel €€€** *1, Herrengassse 12, tel: 01-227 800;* www.radissonhotels.com/en-us/hotels. Very central, chic and well-designed, this 21st-century 'style' hotel is a swish place to stay. The rooms are very comfortable and the facilities excellent. It's also not quite as expensive as it first appears (check out the web 'specials').

**The Ring €€€€** *1, Kärntner Ring 8, tel: 01-22 122;* www.theringhotel.com. This cool but comfy Ringstrasse hotel has been given an intimate designer interior. The good-value classy rooms have a gently modern look, there is a great bistro and bar with a geographically roving wine list, and the hotel has a good day spa with the usual facials and massages.

**Rosewood Vienna €€€€** *1, Petersplatz 7, tel: 01-7999 888;* www.rosewoodhotels.com. Housed in a beautifully restored 19th-century building on one of the most famous squares in the old town, this hotel is luxury at its best. 99 spacious rooms and suites merge past and present through elegant textural and artistic elements. Amenities include the Asaya Spa and state-of-the-art fitness centre.

**Sacher €€€€** *1, Philharmonikerstrasse 4, tel: 01-514 560;* www.sacher.com. Archdukes, ministers and senior army officers used to stay here, and the Sacher is still the city's most famous hotel. Past its heyday, perhaps, but you can still be sure of top-class service. Some of the 152 rooms are accessible to wheelchair users.

**Suzanne €** *1, Walfischgasse 4, tel: 01-513 2507;* www.pension-suzanne.at. Two generations of the Strafinger family have worked to provide homely digs in their spacious apartments with *fin de siècle*-style furnishings. The pension is close to the Opera and city centre.

**Topazz €€€** *1, Lichtensteg 3, tel: 01-532 2250;* www.hoteltopazz.com. Occupying a striking building with oval portholes for windows, this cutting-edge hotel takes the design theme to new heights. Bedrooms are studies in cool styling, all blacks and beiges, quirky lamps and big-print wallpaper – and you can perch in those funky windows to admire the views across town. Enjoy a health-conscious start to the day in the futuristic breakfast room.

**Wandl €€** *1, Petersplatz 9, tel: 01-534 550;* www.hotel-wandl.com. Located immediately behind the Peterskirche (just off Graben), and thus very much at the hub of things. It was built in the 1700s as the residence of a court official, and still retains a historic feel. The rooms are surprisingly contemporary, and rates are reasonable for the facilities on offer.

# AROUND THE RINGSTRASSE (DISTRICTS 2–9)

**Altstadt Vienna €€€** *7, Kirchengasse 41, tel: 01-5226 666;* www.altstadt.at. Housed in a 19th-century apartment block, attentive staff, cutting edge décor and a location within walking distance of most sights make this a sure-fire winner. Room rates include breakfast and afternoon tea, a feature you won't find many other places. Some rooms are in converted apartments with tall windows, double doors and preposterously high ceilings.

**Das Triest €€€** *4, Wiedner Hauptstrasse 12, tel: 01-589 180;* www.dastriest. at. This great little design hotel set the scene for the explosion of chic, contemporary places to sleep in the Austrian capital. An old stable, dating back approximately 300 years, was given a brand-new look by designer Terence Conran producing a characteristic mix of beautifully lit minimalist rooms and restored elements of the original building. There is also a decent Italian restaurant and a great bar.

**Das Tyrol €€** *6, Mariahilfer Strasse 15, tel: 01-587 5415;* www.das-tyrol.at. Located in the Museumsquartier, this boutique hotel has brightly decorated rooms, pristine bathrooms and a breakfast you'll be looking forward to the night before. The hotel is littered with pieces of contemporary art to get you in the mood for Vienna's many museums and galleries.

**Die Josefine €€** *6, Esterhazygasse 33, tel: 01-58870;* www.hoteljosefine.at. For a huge dose of 1920s and 1930s glamour and a wonderful quirky charm, the Josefine offers 49 rooms combining the style of a Viennese Gründerzeit house with modern amenities.

**Hotel Gilbert €€** *7, Breitegasse 9, tel: 01-523 1345;* www.hotel-gilbert.at. Ideally located between the picturesque Spittelberg district and the Museums Quartier, this family run hotel is most hospitable. The inviting entrance is adorned with plants and colourful furniture, and rooms include extra special loft suites. A good buffet breakfast using local quality products is served.

**Haydn €** *6, Mariahilfer Strasse 57–59, tel: 01-5874 4140;* www.haydn-hotel.at. This simple, mid-range pension is located in a noisy area, but is only a few minutes from the city centre by U-Bahn. There is cycle storage space available to guests, and breakfast is included in the reasonable price.

**Indigo Vienna €€** *5, Rechte Wienzeile 87, tel: 01-890 9373;* www.ihg.com. Tucked away just a stone's throw from the vibrant Naschmarkt, this hotel takes inspiration from the secret gardens of the area across the charming terrace, beautiful courtyard and rooftop garden, as well as the comfortable rooms.

**Kugel €** *7, Siebensterngasse 43, tel: 01-5233 355;* www.hotelkugel.at. Good location in the middle of the shopping district, and small, clean rooms. Enthusiastic owners make the experience more enjoyable. Some rooms are equipped for wheelchair use.

**Levante Parliament €€€** *8, Auerspergstrasse 9, tel: 01-228 28100;* www.thelevante-parliament.com. A fantastic design hotel just behind the Parliament, parallel to the Ringstrasse. Set in a building from 1908, originally designed by Secession architect Robert Oerley, the 2006 redesign featuring chic and cosy reds, browns and oranges, as well as specially commissioned photographs by Curt Themessl and glass sculptures by Ioan Nemtoi (for sale if you take a fancy to them), blends in well with the original fabric of the building. The rooms and bathrooms themselves are studies in comfort and understated elegance and the lovely interior courtyard is a great spot for a drink or meal from the hotel's Nemtoi restaurant. In the basement is a soothing sauna and 'wellness' area.

**Mooons €** *4, Wiedner Gürtel 16, tel: 01-96226;* www.mooons.com. The characteristic façade of Mooons awakes curiosity but this great value hotel keeps its promise inside as well. Rooms have smart technology, and the large windows are a bonus. In addition to a quiet courtyard garden, a roof terrace offers panoramic views. Across the road from the train station that takes you to the airport.

**Hotel Rathaus Wien €€** *8, Lange Gasse 13, tel: 01-400 1122;* www.hotelrathaus-wien.at. The perfect juxtaposition of quiet rooms right in the middle of the lively Josefstadt district, with its many small bars. This hotel's particular quirk is that each of the well-designed rooms is named after an Austrian wine maker, and samples of their wines are found in the minibar. Rates tumble in winter.

**Wild €** *8, Lange Gasse 10, tel: 01-4065 174;* www.pension-wild.com. A popular pension in the Josefstadt district with large modern and very clean rooms with or without en suite facilities, leading off a central stairwell. A decent breakfast (included in the price) is served on the ground floor. There are also two apartments with kitchenettes offered in a building directly across the road.

**Zipser €€** *8, Lange Gasse 49, tel: 01-404 540;* www.zipser.at. In a rather grand, century-old Art Nouveau building, this attractive pension has been run with great care by the same family for three generations. Rooms facing the garden are slightly more expensive. Great location just beyond the Ring in the interesting Josefstadt district, a few minutes' walk from the Rathaus and the Inner City.

## FURTHER AFIELD

**Klimt €** *14, Felbigergasse 58, tel: 01-914 5565;* www.klimt-hotel.at. Renovated in a neo-*Jugendstil* style, this hotel offers the unusual option for guests to order special mattresses on request (a nice emphasis on a good night's sleep). It also has a fabulous honeymoon suite with canopied bed. Snack bar with meals available.

**Landhaus Furhgassl-Huber €€** *19, Rathstrasse 24, tel: 01-440 3033;* www.landhaus-fuhrgassl-huber.at. This hotel is at Neustift am Walde, an area of vineyards and *Heuriger* within the city limits. Once the town hall, the fine interior was designed by Walter von Hoessl, one-time stage designer for the State Opera. It has comfortable rooms and is in a lovely, quiet location.

**Parkhotel Schönbrunn €€** *13, Hietzinger Hauptstrasse 12, tel: 01-878 040;* www.austria-trend.at. Very close to the palace and gardens of Schönbrunn, this renovated hotel formerly housed the emperor's guests and is still redolent of the Imperial past. Amenities include Wi-fi and satellite TV and some of the 312 rooms are wheelchair friendly. Rates include a generous breakfast.

**The Rooms €** *22, Schlenthergasse 17, tel: 0664-431 6830;* www.therooms.at. This lovely bed and breakfast is a little way out of the centre in Donaustadt (near to Kagran U-bahn). Just four rooms (for one to three people each), which are beautifully furnished, with views of the garden. An extremely good choice.

**Roomz €** *11, Paragonstrasse 1, tel: 01-7431 777;* www.roomz-vienna.com. Excellent value for a bit of modern comfort, this budget hotel near the Gasometers has 152 spotless rooms with a designer feel, all with contemporary bathrooms attached. There is a pleasant 24-hour bar and restaurant as well.

**Schild €€** *19, Neustift am Walde 97–99, tel: 01-4404 0440;* www.hotel-schild.at. This 28-room hotel is a paradise for anyone who loves wine, since it is surrounded by *Heurigen.* The beautiful country location will also appeal to keen cyclists as the hotel offers both cycle storage and repair facilities. Some wheelchair-friendly rooms are available.

## GUMPOLDSKIRCHEN

**Krug €** *Schulgasse 1, tel: 0699 131-47273;* www.hotel-krug.at. A simply-furnished affordable hotel with 10 rooms, each with en suite bathroom, 20km (12 miles) from Vienna. Breakfast is included in the price.

**Hotel Turmhof €€** *Josef Schöffel Strasse 9, tel: 02252-607 333;* www.hotel-turmhof.at. This modern make-over of a pretty old building makes for attractive large rooms with spacious bathrooms. Most rooms have views over the surrounding vineyards and there is a great rooftop suite.

**Winzerhotel Vöhringer €€** *Wienerstrasse 26, tel: 02252-607 400;* www.winzerhotel.at. A very well-maintained small business hotel with spotless rooms decorated in a modern style. The bathrooms are large and there is a lovely courtyard to sit out in when the weather is pleasant. It is only five minutes' walk to the station for the train into Vienna.

# INDEX

# Vienna Transport

U1 - U6    U-Bahn
—————    S-Bahn
—————    Lokalbahn (Badner Bahn)

●    Station
○ ⬭    Interchange
▢ ⬜    Interchange and terminus
■    Terminus

Tulln a.d. Donau, St. Pölten

S40

Nußdorf

Heiligestadt
U4

Spi

Oberdöbling

Krottenbachstr.

Nußdorfer Str.

Gersthof

Währinger Str.-Volksoper

Fran Jose Bhf.

Hernals

Michelbeuern-AKH

Alser Straße

S45

Josefst Str.

Purkersdorf-Sanatorium

Ottakring U3

Kenderstr.

Hütteldorfer Str.

Josefst str.

Thalias

Schwegler str.

Burgg.-Stadtha

Weidlingau

Haderstorf

Wolf in der Au

Hütteldorf

Breitensee

Neulengbach

S50, 80

S50

U4

Penzing

West-bahnhof

Ober St Veit

Braunschweig.

Gumpendorfer Straße

Marc

Unter St Veit

Hietzing

Schönbrunn

Meidling Haupstr.

Längenfeldg.

Niederl str.

S80

Bahnhof Meidling

Dörfelstr.

Wolfgang

Ei

Speising

S2, 3, 4

Tschertteg

Schedifkapla

Hetzendorf

Am Schöpfwerk

Schöpfwerk

Aterlaa

Gutheil-Schoder-G.

Atzgersdorf

Erlaaer Str.

Inzersdorf Lokalbahn

Perfektastr.

Neu Erlaa

Liesing

Siebenhirten U6

Schönbrunner Allee

Vösendorf-Siebenhirten

Wiener Neustadt

Baden

# THE **MINI** ROUGH GUIDE TO
# VIENNA

**First Edition 2023**

**Editor:** Annie Warren
**Original author:** Jack Altman
**Updater:** Jackie Staddon
**Picture Editor:** Tom Smyth
**Cartography Update:** Katie Bennett
**Layout:** Greg Madejak
**Head of DTP and Pre-Press:** Rebeka Davies
**Head of Publishing:** Sarah Clark
**Photography Credits:** Austria Tourism 15, 30, 46, 51, 79, 88, 93; Britta Jaschinski/Apa Publications 6B, 26, 38, 41, 58, 60, 75, 81, 86, 92, 100, 102, 103; Corbis 42; Dreamstime 22, 52, 66, 84; Elena Schweitzer 37; Fotolia 4ML, 5T, 35, 57, 65, 67, 76; Glyn Genin/Apa Publications 5M, 29, 33, 34, 56, 68, 70, 71, 94; iStock 5T, 5T, 5M, 12, 17, 19, 21, 49, 54, 72, 90, 97, 98, 101; josef muellek 11; Public domain 4TL, 5M, 63; Shutterstock 1, 4ML, 6T, 7T, 7B, 62, 81; Vienna Tourist Board 4BR, 5M, 45, 48
**Cover Credits:** Upper Belvedere **Canadastock/Shutterstock**

### Distribution

**UK, Ireland and Europe:** Apa Publications (UK) Ltd; sales@roughguides.com
**United States and Canada:** Ingram Publisher Services; ips@ingramcontent.com
**Australia and New Zealand:** Booktopia; retailer@booktopia.com.au
**Worldwide:** Apa Publications (UK) Ltd; sales@roughguides.com

### Contact us

Every effort has been made to provide accurate information in this publication, but changes are inevitable. The publisher cannot be held responsible for any resulting loss, inconvenience or injury sustained by any traveller as a result of information or advice contained in the guide. We would appreciate it if readers would call our attention to any errors or outdated information, or if you feel we've left something out. Please send your comments with the subject line "Rough Guide Mini Vienna Update" to mail@uk.roughguides.com.